THE

PRAYER

CENTERED

LIFE

LIVING IN CONVERSATION
WITH THE FATHER

DUDLEY J. DELFFS

NAVPRESS ◑

BRINGING TRUTH TO LIFE
NavPress Publishing Group
P.O. Box 35001, Colorado Springs, Colorado 80935

The Navigators is an international Christian organization. Our mission is to reach, disciple, and equip people to know Christ and to make Him known through successive generations. We envision multitudes of diverse people in the United States and every other nation who have a passionate love for Christ, live a lifestyle of sharing Christ's love, and multiply spiritual laborers among those without Christ.

NavPress is the publishing ministry of The Navigators. NavPress publications help believers learn biblical truth and apply what they learn to their lives and ministries. Our mission is to stimulate spiritual formation among our readers.

© 1997 by Dudley J. Delffs

Library of Congress Catalog Card Number: 97-50346
ISBN 0-89109-997-2

Cover illustration: Linda Montgomery/Irmeli Holmberg

Some of the anecdotal illustrations in this book are true to life and are included with the permission of the persons involved. All other illustrations are composites of real situations, and any resemblance to people living or dead is coincidental.

Unless otherwise identified, all Scripture quotations in this publication are taken from the *HOLY BIBLE: NEW INTERNATIONAL VERSION* ® (NIV®). Copyright © 1973, 1978, 1984 by International Bible Society. Used by permission of Zondervan Publishing House. All rights reserved. Other versions used include: the *New American Standard Bible* (NASB), © The Lockman Foundation 1960, 1962, 1963, 1968, 1971, 1972, 1973, 1975, 1977; the *New Revised Standard Version* (NRSV), copyright 1989, by the Division of Christian Education of the National Council of the Churches of Christ in the USA, used by permission, all rights reserved; *The Message: New Testament with Psalms and Proverbs* by Eugene H. Peterson, copyright © 1993, 1994, 1995, used by permission of NavPress Publishing Group; and the *King James Version* (KJV).

Delffs, Dudley J.
    The prayer-centered life : living in conversation with the Father / Dudley J. Delffs.
        p.   cm.
    ISBN 0-89109-997-2 (pbk.)
    1. prayer. I. Title
    BV210.2.D425   1997
        248.3'2—dc21   96-50346
                                                                         CIP

Printed in the United States of America

1 2 3 4 5 6 7 8 9 10 11 12 13 14 15 / 99 98 97

Published in association with the literary agency of Alive Communications, 1465 Kelly Johnson Boulevard, Suite 320, Colorado Springs, CO 80920.

FOR A FREE CATALOG OF
NAVPRESS BOOKS & BIBLE STUDIES,
CALL 1-800-366-7788 (USA)
or 1-416-499-4615 (CANADA)

CONTENTS

For my girls, Mary Elise and Annie,
and for the Mother of their Beauty, My Wife

ACKNOWLEDGMENTS

This book is the culmination of an extraordinary process of prayer, study, discussion, and the gifts of many invaluable people. I want to thank friends who shared frankly about their own prayer lives and dared me to ask hard questions and enter into silence.

I'm grateful for the support and encouragement of friends like Bill and Lisa Reagan, Doug and Cindy Skilton, John and Sandy Pierce, Darlene Hayes, and Jan Thurmer. I'm indebted to men who continue to love and pray for me even when separated by geography: Jim McClanahan, John Cunningham, Scott Broome, Stephen Seay. And thankfully, Harvey Thurmer, you live in Denver. I thank Gary Stanley for sharing his study on Jesus' prayers in the Scriptures.

For my parents' love and their enthusiastic support, I'm most grateful.

I appreciate the prayers and contributions my colleagues and students at Colorado Christian University made to this endeavor. To Jason Rose for research and conversational stimulus. To Dr. Phyllis Klein, for sustaining gifts of friendship, gentle guidance, thoughts on prayer and poetry, and the Christian journey.

The wonderful staff folks at NavPress deserve special kudos for their continued support and vision for me. Thanks to Steve Webb, Nanci McAllister, and Jack Smith. Liz Heaney deserves special thanks for her caring and thoughtful suggestions and editing. This book would not be what it is without her help.

Kathy Yanni, who I'm privileged to call both friend and comrade in this business of writing. Here's to the many boxes of Macanudos to come.

Finally, I burn with gratitude for the gifts of my girls, Mary Elise and Annie, who delightfully shine like twin beams of the Father's love. I appreciate the sacrifice of time required for me to hole up in the basement and write. Dotti, you are editor, walking concordance, supporter, pray-er, partner, friend, and lover. Your contribution to this book is evidenced by its completion, and yet so much more than what is seen on its pages. Thank you.

STARTING FROM ZERO

When thou prayest,
rather let thy heart be without words
than thy words without heart.

—JOHN BUNYAN

One of the first heartfelt prayers I can remember praying was in second or third grade. My teacher, Miss Hipple, announced that she would give us a surprise quiz shortly, then collected lunch money and took roll.

When we stood for the Pledge of Allegiance, I placed my hand over my heart and mouthed the patriotic words, but inside I prayed the most fervent of prayers. I remember asking God to help me do my best on this terrible, unexpected quiz.

I cautiously answered question after question, waiting for the one that would stop me cold in my ignorance. As it turned out, I scored a hundred. Hey, I'd discovered that prayer works!

Not long after that day, Miss Hipple sprung another pop quiz on our class. Once again I prayed my prayer of panic and hoped for the best. This time I barely passed. At first I was terribly disappointed that God didn't come through for me again. Then I started thinking that maybe I hadn't prayed the right way that second time. Since I attended a Catholic school, I thought maybe I should have tried the Apostles' Creed or the Hail Mary. I'd need to work on that.

Remote-Control Prayers

It feels like I've spent most of my life battling the mentality that prayer is an acquired skill I can master. For a long time I skipped from one method to another, looking for the right and best way to pray. Such a pursuit of prayer reminds me of channel surfing, the way I sometimes find myself jumping from channel to channel, looking for that perfect movie or ball game to engage me. If I'm honest, I know that I'm avoiding my boredom or frustration by continuously clicking the remote control.

It is much the same when we pray without genuinely wanting to engage with the Father. This kind of remote-control prayer allows us to keep up the appearance of prayer without examining why we're doing it. It is so much easier to "click" on to a new book or prayer technique than to examine our hearts and honestly seek to be alone with God.

Even in grade school I knew that my motives played a role in my prayers, and mine were usually mixed. Today many of my prayers still seem selfish and sometimes even trivial. I feel self-conscious when I ask and ask and ask. Or I feel incredibly guilty that my prayer life isn't what it should be; it's one of those things I'll get disciplined about someday— like following a low-fat diet plan or exercise regimen—but I simply don't have the time and energy right now. I don't think I'm alone in this.

In fact, many Christians tell me they're simply too undisciplined to have a consistent prayer life. Recently, the dear mother of a close friend was visiting from Texas. She asked about my writing and what project I was currently pursuing. When I told her it was a book on prayer, she immediately blushed and responded, "Oh, that's just what I need. I hate to admit it, but even though I've been a believer most of my life, prayer is still so hard for me." She said it as if prayer were a skill for which she simply didn't have the required talent or aptitude.

Another friend, who was also a long time Christian, asked me, "Do you think there's a spiritual gift of prayer that allows some people to be better prayer warriors than others?"

"Yes and no," I replied. "I believe it's similar to what Robert Bly said: We're all born poets, but some of us unlearn it as we grow up."

God draws us to communicate with Him through the power of His Word, through the gift of Jesus, through the wonder of watching a thunderstorm bruise the afternoon sky and then heal it with a rainbow. He calls us to engage with Him, but we all respond in different ways, with varying levels of involvement.

Created for Relationship

God created us as relational beings modeled on His triune personality of Father, Son, and Spirit. The Genesis account shows the Creator's desire for relationship and companionship with His holy creation. He created both male and female so they might relate to one another and love one another. This relationship between man and woman is a smaller-scale version of the way He loves us. God talked with Adam and Eve every day, and He confronted them after they did the only thing they had been asked not to do—munch the forbidden Red Delicious.

After our foreparents are exiled from their home, God's communication with them becomes less direct. He speaks through the Law, the prophets, and through divine events, leading up to His gift of Jesus as our bridge back to a more personal, directly relational intimacy with Himself. God dissolves much of the fear and awe that pervades His relationship with His people in the Old Testament by the event of Jesus' death and resurrection, and by giving us the gift of His indwelling Holy Spirit. Thus, in the Old Testament, God's name is unspeakable and His Being reverently feared, while in the New Testament Jesus informs us that we now can graciously call God *Abba,* that is, Father . . . Daddy. We've come full circle. We start at the most intimate of relationships—Creator and creation in the garden—move into the most formal of relationships—Holy One to sinful, fickle people—and back to the most intimate of relationships once again.

This bridge between humanity and holiness is best embodied by Jesus, who knows what it's like to be us, to be flesh and blood, and yet to be God. Through Christ, we have the Perfect Advocate who reestablished our direct line of communication with His Father: "For we do not have a high priest who is unable to sympathize with our weaknesses, but we have one who has been tempted in every way, just as we are—yet was without sin. Let us then approach the throne of grace with confidence, so that we may receive mercy and find grace to help us in our time of need" (Hebrews 4:15-16).

I've discovered that my "time of need" is not only in moments of dire circumstances or emotional lows. My need for my Father is incessant. You and I were made to need God—to relate, share, talk, commune, love Him—always. Consequently, our desire for communication with Him is eternal as well. Prayer is as essential to life as food, water, and air.

Why, then, does prayer seem so difficult? If we don't have to be taught to get hungry or thirsty, why does prayer often seem tedious, pressured, or obligational? Perhaps because we make it that way, because we "unlearn" the poetry of prayer that comes so naturally to us as children and as new believers. There's a childlikeness of spirit, a humble dependence on the Father, that is required in order to grow and mature into the likeness of Christ. Paradoxically, the more dependent we become, the more we grow into mature "adult" Christians.

I think about the way my three-year-old draws pictures for me: "Look, Daddy, I made a green and a blue and a purple and a yellow butterfly for you." In my eyes, she can't get it wrong. Her drawing is deeply and aesthetically pleasing to me, because she's my daughter and I love her and I love her innocent exploration of color, expression, and her world. I believe our heavenly Father holds the same view of us when we honestly and unpretentiously communicate with Him.

Why don't we hold on to this view? I ask you to consider the books and articles you've read and the sermons you've heard on the subject of prayer. How many of them left you hungry and enraptured with desire for your Father? How many of them motivated you to talk passionately to God about everything? How many of them challenged you to explore the uniqueness of your own spiritual color palette of prayer? From my experience, not many. Most give us formulas, patterns of discipline, or reasons why we should pray harder if we really want to call ourselves believers. We end up like my friend's mother, blushing and ashamed, feeling guilt-ridden that we're not better pray-ers. It's akin to the same kind of embarrassment and shame we feel sometimes for not being more mechanically inclined or for being mathematically impaired.

As I perused libraries and bookstores to do research for this book, I found all kinds of prayer techniques and formulas—*Ten Steps from the Lord's Prayer, Why Kneeling Is a Must, How to Pray an Hour a Day.* Don't get me wrong; I'm not categorically dismissing these books. Many of them give practical suggestions about how to enrich our prayer lives. But many of them simply teach a person to go through the obligatory motions: "You are hereby obligated to spend X number of minutes, hours, days in prayer for the rest of your life as a dutiful Christian." Often the implication is that it doesn't matter what we pray or how we pray or how we feel about life and God and ourselves. While I agree that we must be disciplined and consistent in our prayer lives, a contractual mode of prayer only numbs our souls and deadens our hearts to the intimacy we long for.

Starting from Zero

Because we are created for intimacy with our Father, we truly long for a relational connection with God through prayer. If we focus on the method instead of the goal, we are bound to be dissatisfied. A legalistic approach doesn't allow room to struggle, grow, and simply rest in God's love.

This is why we must start from zero every time we pray, not because we have nothing but because *we don't have to have anything to offer to God except our hearts.* "You do not delight in sacrifice, or I would bring it; you do not take pleasure in burnt offerings. The sacrifices of God are a broken spirit; a broken and contrite heart, O God, you will not despise" (Psalm 51:16-17).

A friend confessed to me that the hardest part of prayer for her was to start at zero: "I feel like I need to be holy and perfect, sanctified and ready to enter heaven before I can talk to God. I forget that just the opposite is true. I can talk with Him anytime, no matter where I am or what I've done."

An approach to prayer that focuses on form and ignores content was the essence of the Pharisees' hypocrisy, which sought to follow God's Law through human skill rather than as a loving desire to know and obey the Father.

Our attraction to legalistic prayer remains alive and well today. Recently in a church Sunday school class, several members were asked to speak about how they incorporate prayer and Bible study into their daily lives. The first speaker, a businessman in his thirties, described the techniques he had learned from a previous discipler. Every day he read one psalm and one chapter from the Gospels first thing in the morning, and then spent thirty minutes praying down his list of priorities for that day. The next speaker, an engineer in his forties, described a similar routine. He had a special "prayer day-timer" that reminded him to pray as he scheduled appointments and planned future events. The third speaker, a new Christian for all of six months, described how hard she tried to concentrate on praying every day at exactly the same time, and how terrible she felt if she didn't. "I missed two quiet times this week and just feel awful," she said. "How disappointed and ashamed of me God must be right now!"

The last speaker, a Christian mother and homemaker, said, "I guess I'm here for balance. My prayer times used to be very regimented and structured. Every day I dreaded [prayer time] and felt so relieved when it was over and I could go on with my day. Some of you might describe my quiet times now as a bit too loose or unstructured. And I'll be honest, I sometimes miss a couple of days of regular prayer time. But it doesn't keep me from praying at other times during my day. And it doesn't mean I feel guilty about it, either. In fact, my prayer life changed when someone told me, 'Jesus died so that you don't have to live up to the Law. You can't do it anyway. Pray without ceasing and do it with a passion.' I've felt free to converse with my Father ever since."

Many Christian men and women have rich, passionate prayer lives based on a highly structured format. However, that's not the only way or perhaps not even the best way to commune with God. I say this because each person's faith journey is unique, and we each have a unique, individual prayer life with its seasons, peaks and valleys, means and methods. The key to a rich prayer life lies in exploring the uniqueness of your relationship with your Father.

You do that by starting from where you are every day, every time you pray. In his marvelous book on prayer, Richard Foster calls this "Simple Prayer" and explains, "In Simple Prayer we bring ourselves before God just as we are, warts and all. Like children before a loving father, we open our hearts and make our requests."[1]

Does this sound self-centered? Narcissistic? Often it is. Nonetheless, it's who you are as a fallible man or woman being recrafted into the perfect image of the only unself-centered, holy human—the Son of God.

This kind of direct, honest communication with God again reminds me of my daughter, Mary Elise, when she tells me about her day. "Daddy," she might say, "I played outside with Kaylee today and we went to the park. Mommy and baby Annie came too. I watched *Cinderella* and took a nap . . ." and on and on. Her words reflect the pinball bounces of her thoughts and feelings as she simply basks in being with her daddy at the end of a long day apart from him.

Recently my wife and I watched a TV talk show in which a wife told her husband that he often bored her with his trivial chit chat and insignificant conversations. The husband was obviously hurt. Dotti turned to me and said, "How selfish that seems. How can we truly trust and love one another without the freedom to ramble or discuss trivial, even silly, things?"

I believe the same is true of our conversations with God. While we shouldn't try to ramble or get lost in minutiae, I believe it's okay when we do. The details of my wife's and daughters' day are significant to me, just because those details are on their minds, because they want to tell me about them, because they desire my attention. How much greater is our Father's desire for us to share with Him, even when it seems trivial or "unspiritual" to us. As C. S. Lewis put it, "We must lay before Him what is in us, not what ought to be in us."[2]

If we consider many of the prayers from folks in the Bible, we see that their prayers were often cluttered with mixed motivations and unfocused details. Consider Jacob's fear-based prayer for God to protect him from his rightfully angry brother Esau: "Save me, I pray, from the hand of my brother Esau, for I am afraid he will come and attack me, and also the mothers with their children. But you have said, 'I will surely make you prosper and will make your descendants like the sand of the sea, which cannot be counted'" (Genesis 32:11-12). Jacob's tone borders on a you-got-me-into-this-mess-God, so-you-get-me-out-of-it attitude. He knows his brother's anger is justified and he fears it; yet he also knows what God has promised him. His prayer reflects his fear and confusion.

Or, what about Moses' whiny prayer: "Why have you brought this trouble on your servant? What have I done to displease you that you put the burden of all these people on me?" (Numbers 11:11).

Then there are numerous psalms in which the psalmist delights in the violent retribution God extends to his enemies (Psalms 9,21,35,55,59,64,137, to name a few). Some of the psalms go so far as to beg God to leave the speaker alone! "Remove your stroke from me; I am worn down by the blows of your hand. . . . 'Hear my prayer, O LORD, and give ear to my cry; do not hold your peace at my tears. For I am your passing guest, an alien, like all my forebears. Turn your gaze *away* from me, that I may *smile* again, before I depart and am no more'" (Psalm 39:10, 12-13, NRSV, emphasis added).

God's goodness, power, and patience can more than bear our most honest cry to Him.

Uncommon Prayer

Improving your prayer life means cultivating and uncovering more of your longing for God. Changes in your prayer life emerge as a result of changes in your relationship with God. Prayer then becomes a loving, awe-inspiring conversation with your Abba rather than an empty ritual of going through the motions. God wants our hearts, and one of the essential ways we build our heart relationship with Him is through communication—deep, heart-level honest, engaging dialogues with Him.

This is what we long for most. Why do we resist it? Instead we talk at God, interrupt rather than listen, and withdraw rather than express the raw wounds of our souls. God wants all of us. And relationship with Him is what we want, what we are created for, and *what we are living out, whether we're aware of it or not.* In prayer we express our response to God's presence in our lives. Like the language of poetry, prayer is mysterious, ineffable, inexplicable, simple, timeless, and momentary.

This book examines the basics of prayer from a fresh perspective. When we are reminded that our prayers reflect our hope in God, it simplifies the many pulls we feel to try new techniques and methods. Prayer that comes from the hunger of our hearts ushers us into His presence like a child running to tell her father about her busy day.

Our prayers become love letters home to our Abba Father. His response becomes a loving whisper in the world around us until that time when we can feel His breath in our ear and rest our head on His shoulder.

My prayer is that this book will become a book of uncommon

prayer for you—a way of rekindling the passion you have for Jesus, of refueling and refining the way you speak with the Master and listen to His voice.

PART ONE

AFRAID TO HOPE: BARRIERS TO PRAYER

Prayer is a cry of hope.
—FRENCH PROVERB

Desire is not merely a simple wish;
it is a deep-seated craving;
an intense longing for attainment.
In the realm of spiritual affairs,
it is an important adjunct to prayer.
So important is it, that one might say, almost,
that desire is an absolute essential of prayer.
Desire precedes prayer, accompanies it, is followed by it.
Desire goes before prayer, and by it, is created and intensified.
Prayer is the . . . expression of desire.
—E. M. BOUNDS, *The Necessity of Prayer*

We do not know how to pray as we should,
but the Spirit Himself intercedes for us
with groanings too deep for words.
—ROMANS 8:26 (NASB)

BEYOND BUSYNESS

"Cease striving and know that I am God."
—PSALM 46:10 (NASB)

M y friend Stephen lives over a thousand miles away from me now, up in North Dakota. When he first moved away, we called each other and wrote with spontaneous regularity. As the demands of work, family, church, and life eclipsed my time, I found it more and more difficult to communicate with one of my dearest friends.

My desire is still there; my intent is there, but the actuality lags behind like a bored child. When I do make the time to write to Stephen, it seems that so much has happened in my life that it's impossible to accurately and intimately share my heart's journey over the past few months. Instead, I opt for the convenient, just-the-facts kind of catch-up.

The intimacy of our friendship suffers when we don't communicate and connect at a deeper level, but I'm incredibly fortunate that despite the long yawns of time in between, Stephen challenges me to go below the surface. He's one of those rare friends with whom I can easily reconnect, despite my guilt over lack of frequent communication.

Our communication with God often follows a similar pattern. At times we pray half heartedly on a regular basis so that we can say we're spending time with the Lord. Other times we have rich moments of genuinely experiencing His presence, of listening to Him speak, of feeling the "tendering" of His grace. But these moments are much less frequent, and rarely do they happen according to our timetable. In fact, many of us feel that if we don't have time for the heart-to-heart communication with God that we desire, then we shouldn't pray on the run. When we place such a condition on prayer, our communication with God usually degrades into a lost long-distance relationship.

If we are to grow in love with our Father, we must speak to Him in the midst of our busyness as well as in quiet moments of intimate retreat. This means we start where we are. For most of us, it requires contending with—not eliminating—the busyness in our lives.

Many of the Christians with whom I've discussed this topic tell me they honestly, sincerely desire time to talk with God, but their lives bombard them with demand after demand. These are not people making excuses; they are strong, mature believers I greatly admire and respect. So how do we find time to communicate regularly with our Father? Are there issues beyond busyness that help explain why we never seem to have enough time for Him?

Killing Heart

Despite the conveniences in modern technology or how many times psychologists, counselors, pastors, and teachers tell us to slow down, we are still busy. Most of us know that busyness interferes with having the kind of prayer lives we'd like to have. But such a hectic pace is simply part of modern life, right? Our love and commitment to family, home, job, church, and friends easily consume our lives with both good things and mundane, unless we continually carve out the core of our heart as a garden of prayer and tend it often.

In the Chinese language, the word for *busy* is composed of two characters that symbolize what being busy does: one means "killing," and the other means "heart."

Two kinds of busyness interfere with prayer life, and they both tend to kill our hearts. The first busyness is *external.* We have to work and pay our bills, prepare meals for our families, bathe the kids and change their clothes, serve on church committees, teach Sunday school, change the oil in the car, do the laundry, visit friends, and on and on the eternal litany of the "to-do" list goes. Many, if not most, of these endeavors are very important, some even meaningful, as we go about our days. However, activity is not what motivates us at the center of our being, and we should not allow it to overshadow our heart's true longing.

While some activities and events are pleasurable and significant, our relationships are what get us out of bed in the morning. Activities, events, the motions of our days—all rest on a relational foundation. I get up in the morning and go to work some days because I enjoy what I do and I feel called to it. But I enjoy it and feel called to it because I believe I have something to teach or something to write that might make a difference to my students and readers.

On another level, there are days when I'd give anything not to have to get out of the warm covers next to my wife. But I need to provide for my family; I want to take care of them, protect them, nurture and love them. I want my life to fulfill the purpose God has entrusted to me. While my desire is ultimately in response to love, it brings with it commitment and responsibility. It requires work on my part; it requires sacrifice and suffering.

We must constantly remind ourselves of this relational foundation to our lives in order to fend off the busy activities that would consume us. Otherwise, we live the old paradox of staying so busy for others that we're never present for them. We allow the activities to eclipse the person. "Honey, I'm only working this hard to provide for you and the kids" or "As soon as I get this promotion, I'll have more time to spend in my quiet times with the Lord."

There will always be some urgent activity that begs for our attention. We must consistently choose to remember relationships first.

The second busyness is *internal*; it affects the spirit. In our "Overnight Express"-paced world, busyness of activity seems inevitable. However, busyness of spirit occurs when we allow activities and accomplishments to become more important than relationships or use our busyness to justify withdrawing from relationships. In fact, we may not be very busy with activities at all, but by refusing to meet God in the quiet stillness of our hearts, we seek out all kinds of diversions and create a restlessness within. This internal busyness causes us to dim our true longings for relationship with others and with our Father.

Sometimes we use busyness as an emotional buffer. Our frantic here-and-there motions allow us to avoid the pain and disappointment inherent in relationships—even in our relationship with God. At the same time our busyness allows us to feel sorry for ourselves. We become self-conscious of our service and want to be rewarded for it (or at least have others work just as hard). We become martyrs in our own minds because we have tangible proof that we love God and work hard to serve Him. Taken to extreme, we start to live in a kind of merit system, not a love relationship founded on grace.

Most of us know that it's not our service God is concerned with. Rather, He's concerned with the condition of our hearts. As the perfect Being He is, if God were to judge us on our own merits—how much and how well we accomplish for Him versus how many times we fail, screw up, or disappoint Him—it would not be a very even scale. My best and most selfless accomplishments could never balance, let alone outweigh my selfish acts, thoughts, and betrayals on any given day.

When we use busyness to keep us from spending time alone with God, we rob ourselves of the very thing we long for most.

Only One Thing Is Necessary

Throughout His life Jesus reinforced the truth of the importance of relationships. He made time for children, foreigners, adulterers, and tax collectors. Out of an endless sea of activity—teaching, preaching, healing—He focused on people first. He calls us to live by the same standard. Perhaps this is best exemplified in His visit with Mary and Martha:

> As Jesus and his disciples were on their way, he came to a village where a woman named Martha opened her home to him. She had a sister called Mary, who sat at the Lord's feet listening to what he said. But Martha was distracted by all the preparations that had to be made. She came to him and asked, "Lord, don't you care that my sister has left me to do the work by myself? Tell her to help me!"

"Martha, Martha," the Lord answered, "you are worried
and upset about many things, but only one thing is needed.
Mary has chosen what is better, and it will not be taken
away from her." (Luke 10:38-42)

First, notice that Martha followed the traditional custom of caring
for her guest by preparing for His stay. She displayed respect, kindness,
and hospitality by cooking a meal and preparing a place for Jesus to rest.
In fact, according to her culture, she was honoring the relationship first.
However, Martha betrayed her self-interest in her question to Jesus.
Notice that Martha knew the answer — she knew that Jesus cared about
her and would not want her "serving" alone. If she were truly interested
in caring about her guest, it wouldn't have mattered that she was doing
it by herself. By asking the question, Martha implied that she would
rather be doing what Mary was doing, or else make sure that Mary
didn't enjoy something Martha could not. To Martha, Jesus didn't seem
to appreciate her efforts enough and was far too tolerant of her sister's
laziness.

Jesus' reply was simple and direct and defied the cultural custom.
He reminded Martha of true priorities. The details of her life — cooking bread, cleaning, starting the fire, mending the cloaks, sweeping,
gathering water, tending animals, gathering vegetables — overshad-
owed why she performed those very acts. And notice Jesus' words: "only
a few things are necessary, really *only* one." The contrast between
Martha's concern for "so many things" and the emphasis on "only" is
deliberately pointed. Because of her limited view, Martha may not have
even realized what she was missing. Mary, however, saw a larger vista,
realized her options, and chose based on her priority: to know and love
her Lord.

We, like Martha, often lose sight of the relationship goal, even as
we attempt to make our relationships a priority. Technology can often
be a good thing that frees up our time for the people we care about,
but often we use it to cram in more things to do. What good are all
the fax machines, cell phones, laptops, and pagers in the world if they
obscure our vision to the point that we don't realize what we're truly
missing? Too often we bask in serving all the people in our lives but

never simply *being* with them—talking, loving, engaging our hearts with theirs.

This is especially true of the relationship we claim matters most to us—our commitment to love and follow Christ. Again, like Martha, we view our service to God as evidence of our commitment—we teach at church, serve on committees, lead prayer services, help out with music, contribute money, attend services. We may even be full-time pastors and ministers. Yet all of us know that busyness often produces a martyr's attitude with an angry edge: If we're working so hard serving You, God, why aren't we enjoying any of the relational benefits that are supposed to come with knowing You? Why is it still so hard to be alone with You, to pray honestly and deeply from the wellspring of our being? Like the elder son in the parable of the prodigal in Luke 15, we resent those who often seem less responsible or involved in ministry yet seem to know the Father in a simpler, more direct kind of way. We forget that we have full access to our Father's attention and love all the time.

Heavenly Graffiti

If our relationship with God is our motivation for prayer, then we will sustain the dialogue even when our lives are incredibly full. In fact, if I allow it, my busyness often reminds me of how desperately I long to be alone with my Father. Out of my chaotic busyness, my Father takes the edge off the sword of the urgent and replaces it with His healing, loving presence.

I experienced this at the end of last semester when my wife gave me a present. She sent me away, alone, to a mountain retreat center located near the top of a fourteen-thousand-foot peak.

I arrived late in the afternoon and was graciously greeted and given my choice of rooms. I chose the Blue Spruce room in the back right corner of the upper level. It had a worship-inspiring view of a snowy mountain slope dominated by a towering example of my room's namesake. I unpacked, reviewed the facilities, and had a snack. I began to organize my stay and schedule the times I would write, read, pray, hike, and sleep. Then I stopped and stared at the big lonesome spruce beyond my double window. Something struck me as terribly wrong about my schedule. So I scrapped it.

For the next two days I wandered at the Holy Spirit's guidance. I still ended up doing most of the activities that were on my list, but not just to check them off. Instead I spontaneously sought God's presence. I ate when I was hungry and slept when tired. Throughout the weekend I talked to God and listened for His replies. I found Him in both expected and unexpected places.

First I met Him in the tiny prayer closet outside my room. I've appreciated the purpose of such spaces, but they've always made me feel a bit spiritually claustrophobic. How could time in such a confined space lead to the open expanse of green-meadow freedom I longed for with God? This room was different. The small kneeler faced a water-color sketch of Noah's ark beneath a band of rainwashed colors. Beneath the boat the artist had written Genesis 9:12 in calligraphy: "This is the sign of the covenant which I am making between Me and you and every living creature that is with you. I set my bow in the cloud and it shall be a sign . . ." As I looked up at the rainbow again, I noticed a small white dove returning to the ark with a jade green olive branch clenched in its beak. It was a peace sign, a symbol of hope and renewal, a new beginning.

I quickly poured out my heart to God and voiced all the weary complaints I harbored from my busy life. There was a sense of His patient listening, and that felt wonderfully refreshing, but there was also a greater sense of rekindling the relationship, of greeting someone I love dearly and haven't seen in a great while.

It was an embracing, a rebonding that stilled me from all the inner turmoil that had been flooding my soul for the past months. I left the prayer chapel with that odd kind of peace that causes one to revel in silence, to seek out aloneness, to want more of the Father's presence.

The other most significant time for me occurred the next afternoon. The weather, sunny and mild, beckoned me beyond the slopes just outside my window. I had the peculiar sensation that I was keeping an appointment. I put on my hiking boots and set off through the snowy underbrush and pine-scented air. As I hiked further, the snow got deeper and deeper—up to my knees at times. Despite not having on gaiters, I didn't get very cold this December day. The blue clear sky urged me on as if I would find spring on the other side of the next hill.

After about an hour or so, I found myself absorbed by my sur-roundings—the small creek of snow run-off, the canopy of towering pines and evergreens, the crisp carpet of white that blanketed every step. I found myself talking to my Father with ease and familiarity. I felt very unself-conscious and let my heart words ramble from thought to thought. Like a tired child, I finally ran out of things to say and simply listened. A blackbird cawed from a treetop. A plane droned across the sky to my right. I was overcome with a sense of marvel at God's pres-ence in me and my surroundings.

His message to me seemed very simple. I took my walking stick and began writing two-foot-high block letter words in the snowy hill-side. JOY, I inscribed, followed by PEACE—a kind of heavenly graf-fiti. It seems rather foolish now to try to describe it, and maybe I shouldn't even try. That entire afternoon became a prayer vigil for me. The busyness of spirit I usually allowed to dictate my heart was replaced once more by the Spirit of God, a dove descending with an olive branch back to my sinking ship of frenzied activity.

Those times are rare and as precious as pearls, and I can't pretend to understand how to make them happen. But throughout my life I've been graced with several such times, as most of us are, and they do seem to have a few things in common.

Usually they happen when we step back from the immediacy of our surroundings and take in the whole panorama, not just the urgent clamoring before us. In essence, we start from where we are by letting go of guilt, confessing our true desire to spend time with God, and our failure always to pursue Him before other things. "Cease striving and know that I am God," the psalmist instructs (46:10 NASB).

The peace I experienced that day on my snowy hike was more than just some transcendental response to the beauty of nature. It was the antithesis of my busyness of spirit, the opposite of Martha's frenetic spirit of service. It was the peace that Christ left with us on the eve of His death as an earnest of what was to come. "Peace I leave with you; my peace I give you. I do not give to you as the world gives. Do not let your hearts be troubled and do not be afraid" (John 14:27). We need to hold onto those times of deep connection as we reenter the activities we're called to do.

The peaceful moment of my solitude with God on that snowy mountain is just a memory now. I'm back in the throes of teaching, appointments, and deadlines. Yet the memory of that afternoon, the holy absurdity of my carving words in the snow as if I were a boy on the beach, connects to the peace Christ spoke of. It is a peace beyond circumstance, a relational connection to the living God, the Holy Spirit breathing blessed fire in us, fanning the love that is the kingdom of God within us.

We will always, all of us, be *busy,* in both the physical and spiritual sense of the word. There will always be tasks, chores, bills, crises, and blessed moments of quiet in between. There will always be the temptation to seek out or adopt legalism and busyness as ways of feeling good about our spirituality—"See all that I've done for you, God." We must not let busyness mask the true business at hand—our moving deeper in love and further into relationship with the Trinity of God the Father, Jesus the Son, and the Spirit of Life. This is our heart's true longing, the place from which all our prayers arise.

Questions for Prayer and Reflection

As you think through what it means to seek God where you are, not where you want to be or think you should be, the following questions may prove helpful. Feel free to answer all of them or only one. You may want to go to a favorite chair in your home, or you may want to take a walk through a park or wood. If it helps, write your thoughts in a journal as you seek to still yourself before God.

1. Describe your relationship with God right now—intimate, distant, dry, pleasant, difficult, joyful, painful—reflect on all the adjectives that come to mind. Where are you starting from? How does your prayer life reflect this relational place?

2. List all the things you can think of that take you away from time you'd like to spend praying. How many of these things are essential and how many simply become excuses not to seek conversation with God?

3. Try to identify your own spirit of busyness, the ways that you become a Martha in order to feel like a "good Christian." Ask God to calm your heart and reveal to you what things are really essential, "really only *one*," as Jesus said.

4. Try writing a poem (you don't have to be a poet!) that expresses the moments you have felt the peace of Christ that passes all understanding. Be as concrete and specific as you can—where you were, what you felt, who you were with, sensual details of sight, sound, smell, taste, touch.

5. Read through Psalm 23. Personalize it by rewording to fit your life experiences into the text. Contrast your most difficult moments (trials, disappointments, fears, tragedies—those "valley of the shadow" seasons of life) with your most joyful moments of trusting God and tasting His goodness. Be as specific as you can.

6. Complete this sentence: "My heart's true longing is . . ." What would you like to have happen inside you during the course of reading this book?

———

God of all grace, give us your peace that passes
understanding, that the quietness that comes from
friendliness with human beings, and true divine friendship
with you may possess our soul; that we, withdrawn awhile
from the turmoil of the world, may gather the strength that we
have lost, and established and strengthened
by your grace, pass on through all the troubles of this earthly
life, safe into the haven of eternal rest; through Jesus Christ
our Lord. Amen.[1]

—GEORGE DAWSON

PRAYING
IN THE DARK

*Why, O Lord, do you reject me
and hide your face from me?*

PSALM 88:14

*You have put me in the lowest pit,
in the darkest depths.*

PSALM 88:6

As my daughter approached her third birthday, my wife and I decided it was time for her to give up the pacifier. Used only at bedtime, Mary Elise's "pappy" was a security, a familiar way to lose herself to sleep. We prayed for parental wisdom, my wife did a little research, and we came up with a plan. We took all of Mary Elise's pappies, sealed them in a plastic bag, and let her hand them over to the woman behind the counter at Toys-Я-Us. Then she picked out a toy in exchange for relinquishing one of her most beloved possessions. At the time, Mary Elise was unfazed, and quite happy about it.

Bedtime was a different story. Mary Elise begged for her pappies and cried when we reminded her that she'd given them to the cashier at the toy store. We prayed bedtime prayers, and at the end my wife said, "Jesus, please help Mary Elise. Comfort her as she grows up and gives up her pappies. Amen."

"Will Jesus bring back my pappies?" Mary Elise asked.

"No," we said. "But He will make you feel better. He'll comfort you with His presence."

Only a few sniffles as she turned this over in her head. We said goodnight and proceeded to put our other daughter down for the night. About thirty minutes later we heard Mary Elise sobbing in her room. We went in, and she looked up at us and said, "I don't like Jesus very much."

We were speechless. Then we realized she was honestly confronting her pain and grief at a level of honesty most of us rarely face. Most of us "unlearn" what it means to suffer our prayers. Part of me longed to burst into tears and grab my daughter and say, "I know exactly how you feel. Some days I don't much like Him either."

Instead I whispered, "That's okay," and hugged her close. My wife tucked her in, Mary Elise settled down, and we crept out of her room.

"I Don't Feel Like Praying"

Mary Elise's honesty made me reexamine my own emotional response when God doesn't come through. I considered how often I simply don't feel like praying, and the voices of many Christian friends with similar sentiments echoed in my mind. I realized that if starting from where we are—regardless of what that looks or feels like—is the first stride toward connecting with our Father, then sifting through our conflicting emotions must be the next.

Often when I don't feel like praying it's because I don't want to be disappointed. Some days my faith feels strong and I pray more expectantly and confidently. Other days I recall unanswered prayers, or prayers where it feels like Jesus leaves me painfully disappointed with His response.

I don't like questioning God's sense of timing, wisdom, or goodness. And while theologically I trust in those qualities in my mind, my experiences often lead my heart to balk. I allow my fears of the future to intercept my feeble impulses to pray hopefully, expectantly, passionately. Since God doesn't provide the immediate guarantees I crave, my anger boils up like clouds of smoke, obscuring my desire to trust in the One who loves me most. Typically, I justify my silent withdrawal from Him. My doubts multiply; I wonder about His involvement in my life, His concern for my well-being, the flimsiness of my faith, which seems to bend so easily.

Into this murky emotional stew the voice of my heart dims to a whisper. I refuse to pray because it's a futile endeavor that only sets me up for more heartache and letdowns. Rarely do I embrace faith over feelings and circumstances. It's a problem we all face that stems from the way we view prayer. Most of us tend toward extremes. We view prayer as a daily habit that's good for us—a spiritual dental floss, or a pleasant exchange as we drink our morning coffee or stall in traffic, or maybe as an obligation that must be performed with regularity. Maybe we view prayer as something we practice out of desperation, à la Indiana Jones ("I'm not a praying kind of person, but if You're up there God, I really need You to help me out of this jam").

These views not only distort true prayer, they also limit it. When we confine prayer to what feels appropriate, what we've been taught is appropriate, and by our own selfish pride, rarely do we feel the freedom to pray honestly from our present position. We have to wait for the anger, fear, jealousy, envy, frustration, disappointment, or any of the other unpleasant emotions we experience as humans, to subside before we can talk to God.

If we examine Scripture and the examples of the saints, as well as Christ's example, we find that prayer must begin with emotional honesty. We know that God sees through all our smoky illusions and passive withdrawals. He knows what we feel and why we feel that way. Yet we still refuse to cry to Him, question Him, doubt Him, or yes, even yell at Him, because it feels too terrifying, too disrespectful, too raw.

But that's exactly what He asks of us. In fact, when we hide our true feelings from Him, when we sulk or go through the motions of prayer without engaging our hearts first, then we show much more disrespect than if we let it all out to Him. Let's consider some examples.

Cries of the Soul

Time and time again we see the psalmist, often David, pouring out grief, anger, fear, and frustration to his Lord. In Psalm 6:2-3 David writes, "Be merciful to me, LORD, for I am faint; O LORD, heal me, for my bones are in agony. My soul is in anguish. How long, O LORD, how long?" David not only feels the freedom to express the chronic throb of his heart, but he questions God about how long it will last. Psalm 10:1 finds the psalmist asking, "Why, O Lord, do you stand far off? Why do you hide yourself in times of trouble?"

How often do we question the Almighty? Of course it's incredibly presumptuous and arrogant of us, but it's just as prideful to deny that those angry questions never well up within us. Our questions allow us to release the toxic emotions that pollute our perceptions. The psalmist shows us that God listens to our darkest doubts and can handle our negative emotions. But before many of us can feel free to vent at God, we must first realize that our negative emotions are inevitable. We can't control feeling them; emotions are spontaneous poems from the honest core of us. We live in an imperfect world, an in-between state of being perfected. Therefore, we will continue to sense unpleasant, undesirable emotions at the most inappropriate times.

How we act on those emotions, however, is within our control. We can feel what we're feeling without necessarily having to be a slave to it. This includes questioning God with our often petty and shallow questions, as well as questioning Him with our often profound questions and heart-wrenching doubts.

We work so hard to present our best selves to God, our child-at-the-piano-recital-performing-for-our-parents selves. But He accepts and embraces the terrible discords in us as well. In fact, it's crucial to our relationship that we know He accepts *all* of us. How can He redeem us if He isn't allowed into the darkest parts of our lives? Of course He's present in them through the Holy Spirit, if we have chosen to accept His gift. But relationally speaking, we are fragmenting and dividing ourselves if we don't acknowledge our fears, trials, and temptations.

Necessary Temptations
Scripture is consistently clear that while God wants us to avoid known temptations, He also allows us to be tempted. Jesus instructs His disciples to "watch and pray so that you will not fall into temptation" (Matthew 26:41). Paul exhorts us to "avoid every kind of evil" (1 Thessalonians 5:22). Along with this we know that "God is faithful; he will not *let* you be tempted beyond what you can bear. But when you are tempted, he will also provide a way out so that you can stand up under it" (1 Corinthians 10:13, emphasis added).

In Matthew 4:1 we find that "Jesus was *led by the Spirit* into the desert to be tempted by the devil" (emphasis added). Why would our Father who loves us so allow us to face the painful tension of choosing between our flesh and His Spirit, again and again? Why does God allow temptations?

He allows them in order to remind us of our need for Him, of our dependence on His power to overcome the trial, of our love relationship with Him whose passion burns deeper and brighter than the momentary flare-up of selfish opportunity. Too often we allow our pride and self-sufficiency to keep us from running to our Father's arms and humbling ourselves in His embrace by asking for His loving guidance and protection.

While this notion of "necessary" temptations makes us uncomfortable, it also forces us to acknowledge the way we seek to make Christianity safe and comfortable. So often contemporary believers work hard to insulate themselves from the realities of life on earth by over-spiritualizing their lives. (As C. S. Lewis once said in a radio interview, "The greatest detriment to Christianity in the twentieth century is organized religion.") Since Christ saves us from the consequences of our own selfish desires and sinful inclinations, we want to believe that we are now above being human. While we will one day be sanctified with God in heaven, we are not yet. We still struggle, wrestle, and work out our salvation with fear and trembling (Philippians 2:12). In fact, I believe that accepting Christ reawakens and intensifies the longing of what we are created for: life with God. Our yearning becomes acute and "we ourselves, who have the firstfruits of the Spirit, groan inwardly as we wait eagerly for our adoption as sons, the redemption of our bodies" (Romans 8:23).

Philip Yancey, in his column for *Christianity Today,* wrote an excellent article on the "groanings" precipitated by delayed gratification.[1] As he notes, this is foundational to the Christian life; our hope sustains us through this life for the splendor of the next. Yancey also points out that this opposes our present Zeitgeist in which we want our desires satisfied as soon as we can identify them: microwave food, faxed contracts, to-the-minute coverage of world events.

This same tension, often manifested in our prayer lives, draws us toward God and His kingdom and continually increases our appetite for Him, or else we resist this acute yearning and pull away, anesthetizing ourselves through self-centered, more immediate gratification. Unfortunately, we often choose to dull our awareness of pain and suffering, of longing for something more, rather than face it and cry out to God. Counselor and author Dan Allender explains, "It is far easier to snuff out desire with the shroud of despair than to live with the ache of deferred desire."[2]

Sustaining prayer must be honest prayer. No pretense of "appropriate" feelings, no forced civility on our part, but the raw unspoken cries of our hearts in the midst of suffering. While we have no right to question God, to shout at Him, to shake our fist in His face, these responses express the passion of our relationship with Him much more honestly and effectively than pretending that we don't want to feel and do those things. It is much more prideful and presumptuous on our part to "weaken" God by praying as though He can't handle the darts we would sling His way. Honest responses—including cries of despair, shouts of rage, and whispers of fear—pave the way to a more trusting, mature response. We will likely feel the same emotions, yet we will trust Him, because we know He has our best interest at heart, not our immediate comfort or convenience.

Praying Through the Darkness

Perhaps there is no more contemporary example of essential prayer in the midst of horrendous circumstances than that of Job, the man who lost everything. Job's prayers almost crackle with the anger, fear, and sense of betrayal he feels: "Why did I not perish at birth, and die as I came from the womb? . . . Why is light given to those in misery, and life to the bitter of soul, to those who long for death that does not come, who search for it more than for hidden treasure" (Job 3:11,20-21). Later, he says, "I loathe my very life; therefore I will give free rein to my complaint and speak out in the bitterness of my soul. I will say to God: Do not condemn me" (Job 10:1-2).

Philip Yancey, citing Job as the Bible's prime example of disappointment with God, explains:

. . . Job wanders as close to blasphemy as he can get—just to the edge. His words have a startlingly familiar ring because they are so modern. He gives voice to our most deeply felt complaints against God. But chapters 1 and 2 [of Job] prove that, regardless of what Job thinks, God is not on trial in this book. Job is on trial. The point of the book is not suffering: Where is God when it hurts? The prologue dealt with that issue. The point is faith: Where is Job when it hurts?[3]

The book of Job is packed with so many theological and existential issues and questions that entire books have been written around the question of why God allows suffering, why we have pain in our world. I want to focus on one truth: Job remains in communication with God, despite the fact that he feels abandoned and cut off from Him for no apparent reason. Job lives through a nightmare and prays through the darkness in search of restorative light. Imagine that your best friend suddenly stopped returning calls and that your letters returned unopened. Imagine that your life was in shambles and that you needed that best friend now more than ever. If we magnify that example a hundred times, we have a small inkling of what Job must have experienced.

But Job's trials reveal his faith, his willingness to hope, to act on that hope, to keep praying to God, to keep believing that God had not abandoned him and that eventually he would be restored. In one sense, the concept of justice serves as a catalyst to Job's reaction. His life has suddenly been ripped away from him for no reason.

Don't we feel this way at times? How about when our child is diagnosed with leukemia, or we lose our job, or our spouse has an affair—isn't "Why me?" the first question we ask?

The night before his death Jesus asked a variation of this question: "My Father, if it is not possible for this cup to be taken away unless I drink it, may your will be done" (Matthew 26:42). Although Jesus doesn't ask, "Why me?" He does ask, "Is there another way?" Then His steadfast trust in His Father leads Him, even in His darkest hour, to submit to the Father's plan and vision for the way things should work.

In a similar manner, Job, despite his friends' accusations and the despair of his grief and anger, asserts his integrity and honestly beseeches God to deal with him. Despite the fact that Job's fortunes are restored and God responds to him at the end of the book, I won't pretend that the story has a fairy-tale ending. There's still a nagging sense of Job's faith being tested, of God allowing Satan to take away the many blessings in Job's life to see how he would respond to God under those circumstances.

Many scholars point to Job's desire for relationship with God, despite what God can do for him, as the theme of the book. In other words, will Job love God for who He is, rather than for what He does for him? It's the difference between an obligational, contractual business deal and a passionate, fiery interdependence.

In his book *Disappointment with God*, Yancey reminds us that our world is full of unseen, spiritual battles we simply can't perceive or appreciate from our limited viewpoint. Thus, he concludes, "Job teaches that at the moment when faith is hardest and *least* likely, then faith is needed most."[4]

The same is true for prayer. When we least feel like praying, we often need it the most. If we'll admit it, we long to cry out to God, to flood Him with our storm of tears and questions, to release the pent-up anger and doubt and experience the comfort of His embrace. We long to allow Him to still us with a powerful bear hug even as we kick and scream for Him to let us go. We want Him to remind us of how much He loves us, of how He's taken care of us in the past.

Choosing to Seek Him

We observe a similar mindset in the psalmists' cries of despair. The questions, doubts, and fears serve to unclog the emotional floodgates. Like Job's cries, the psalmists' questions are not used to justify withdrawing from God. Rather the questions free the psalmist to act on faith and not give up on God. Faith is not conditional on whether the questions are answered. The psalmist asks the questions and then goes on to remember past times when God revealed Himself, when He proved faithful, when He answered prayer.

The psalmist chooses to embrace the tension of loving and seeking God in a world where we presently only experience glimpses of

Him. Psalm 10 concludes with these words: "The LORD is King for ever and ever; the nations will perish from his land. You hear, O LORD, the desire of the afflicted; you encourage them, and you listen to their cry, defending the fatherless and the oppressed, in order that man, who is of the earth, may terrify no more" (Psalm 10:16-18).

What strikes me is that the psalmist trusts that God is listening to him, even though his question may not be answered or may not be answered in the way he would hope. The psalmist also says that our fear arises because we are "of the earth." We are limited in our perspective on the way God is orchestrating our individual dramas into a divine epic. We only see a small scene of a much larger act. Occasionally we're granted peeks behind the curtain, but only occasionally, and then we often can't comprehend and appreciate what we see. Nevertheless, I believe it's essential to record and consistently remember those times when we see God redeeming an experience or shaping our lives.

A Peek Behind the Curtain

One of the worst periods in my life was the summer after I became a Christian. I had grown up in church and attended a Catholic school. I knew all the Bible stories and had won numerous "sword drills" throughout many months of Sunday schools. I knew what it meant to be a follower of Christ; I had even gone through the motions after being cajoled by a youth worker. But in the midst of my home where my father battled the dark tang of whiskey and I felt all alone, I withheld trusting my heart with anyone or anything, including God. All that to say, when I became a Christian in college, it was after several spiritually prodigal years.

The summer I became a Christian, I found rich fellowship with an especially vital campus ministry group. One of the group leaders, Tad, who had led me to Christ, got me a summer job at a church camp. I was thrilled. Not only could I escape the small-town doldrums and home life blues that had filled previous summers, I would be with a tight-knit group of other Christian college students. We would swim, pray, laugh, and minister to our twelve-year-old charges. What could be better? I had become a Christian and now it felt like God was rewarding me for accepting His love for me.

I got to the camp and gratefully thanked God for such a provision; it was even more than I'd hoped. The other camp counselors were outgoing and dynamic. The camp director, a big blond bear of a man named John, seemed to like me.

The first couple of weeks of camp training (before the campers actually came) raced by. The day before we were to be presented to the church (a mega-church of almost two thousand members) for a dedication, John directed our Bible study around our qualifications for ministry leadership, especially around the qualifications for deacon outlined in 1 Timothy 3. I listened attentively and felt that I met the qualifications as best I could through the grace of God and the blood of Jesus. Then John began talking about what it meant to be "above reproach" (1 Timothy 3:2). He dwelt on sexual sins and immorality, an area where I had stumbled numbly prior to becoming a believer.

I was troubled for the rest of the afternoon. I asked to speak to John after supper and told him what my life had been like before I had embraced Christ. He said I could not stay on as a camp counselor; I had until dawn the next morning to pack my clothes and be gone before the other counselors awoke. He would make an "appropriate explanation" to them. I pleaded with him to let me stay, to let me take on other, lesser, responsibilities. He refused.

A tornado of rage funneled inside me. I had never considered that I might be asked to leave, that I would be considered unfit for ministry. I felt ashamed, spiritually disabled and malformed. That night I sat up in the lifeguard tower twelve feet above the dock and the dark placid lake below. I sat there several hours with a face as wet as the water below me. I tried to figure it out. I could not reason it. I cried out. I questioned.

I packed my laundry duffel bag that read "Dirty Job, But Somebody's Gotta Do It" with my clothes and loaded it into the trunk of my old blue Ford, just as the sky was lightening its way to sunrise. I wept as I drove down the rutted camp road. I returned home to my parents, refused to explain why I had quit my job as camp counselor, and felt relieved that things couldn't get any worse. But they did. My father, after an extended spell of sobriety, disappeared for several weeks. My mother worried herself sick over whether to care or not to care about my father and his whereabouts. I simply numbed myself to the point where I no longer felt. There was no one to talk to; all my friends were away at college or summer jobs. I felt abandoned, forlorn, betrayed.

It took a while for me to get on with my life. My father eventually returned. He became sober again and has remained so. My mother forgave him and they are perhaps happier now than they've ever been. I endured the summer, and gradually over the course of the twelve years since then have forgiven the summer as well. In fact, I eventually rewrote that summer in a somewhat autobiographical novel called *Forgiving August*. Many of the events I changed, but the emotional anguish and disillusionment I felt is reflected in my character, Bounty's, turmoil.

It wasn't until the novel was published and I was forced to talk about its origin in various interviews that I realized I might never have become a writer, something I dearly love and feel called to, if not for that night spent alone in the dark, high atop a bleak tower of despair. Even if I would have become a writer by other means, the relationship between those two events seems like a quick peek behind God's curtain, a glimpse at His redemptive vision of an entire life, not just a single summer of it.

Events such as these remind me that God longs for us to express the depth of our passion for Him right alongside our darkest fears and most violent rages toward Him. Certainly He's capable of handling our emotions, if only we allow Him the opportunity. So often, we act as if we're "protecting" God by refusing to express our honest emotions to Him. While we often interact with each other this way—repressing emotions and avoiding conflict—it's not what God desires from us.

I don't have all the answers to why terrible things happen in our world. I know the right answers theologically and logically, but when I see crack babies born into a life of physical suffering and abandonment, or when I watch my fourteen-year-old niece succumb to the twilight of cancer, then my right answers don't mean very much. What I am sure of is that God can handle my uncertainty, my disappointment, my fear, and my anger. He loves me enough to let me yell at Him if that's what I need to do to keep on trusting Him. He loves you that much too.

Questions for Prayer and Reflection

As you think, pray, or journal through the following questions, trust that God knows your deepest feelings, longings, and uncertainties, and He wants to discuss them with you.

1. What struggle or trial presently impedes your prayer life? How do you feel about this struggle and your relationship with God? Write Him a letter, honestly pouring out the thoughts and feelings of your heart. Trust that He can handle all of them.

2. Read Lamentations 3:19-38. What does this stir in you? How has God revealed His mercy and faithfulness to you in the past? In the present?

3. Perhaps right now you can't relate to Job or to difficult feelings like doubt, disappointment, or pain. Give thanks and reflect on past times when God brought you through trying times to where you are now.

4. What's your greatest disappointment in life right now? What would you like to see God do in this area? Why? Examine your motives and converse with your Father about them.

5. Recall a dark time in your life that you later saw redeemed, at least in part, through God's goodness. Can you thank Him for having a larger, more far-reaching vision for your life than you have?

—

*Dear Lord, today I thought of the words of
Vincent van Gogh: "It is true there is an ebb and flow,
but the sea remains the sea." You are the sea. Although I experience many ups and downs in my emotions and often feel
great shifts and changes in my inner life, you remain the
same. Your sameness is not the sameness of a rock, but the
sameness of a faithful lover. Out of your love I came to life; by
your love I am sustained, and to your love I am always called
back. There are days of sadness and joy; there are feelings of
guilt and feelings of gratitude; there are moments of failure
and moments of success;
but all of them are embraced by your unwavering love.*

*My only real temptation is to doubt in your love,
to think of myself as beyond the reach of your love, to remove
myself from the healing radiance of your love.
To do these things is to move into the darkness of despair.*

*O Lord, sea of love and goodness, let me not fear
too much the storms and winds of my daily life,
and let me know that there is ebb and flow
but that the sea remains the sea.*[5]

—HENRI NOUWEN

AFRAID TO HOPE

"Hope" is the thing with feathers —
That perches in the soul —
And sings the tune without the words —
And never stops — at all —

—EMILY DICKINSON

Recently, my wife Dotti, along with our parents and families, asked me for my Christmas list. This is usually a request I'm more than happy to oblige. It means I get to go through catalogs such as Orvis, J. Crew, Eddie Bauer, Levenger's, as well as take inventory for books and CDs. It means I get to dream and wallow in delusions of getting, certainly not all of these, but even some. I can speculate and re-speculate on which configuration of gifts I'll receive and which ones will come up on the list again next year.

But something was different this year. My heart wasn't in it. When I finished my list, I looked it over and let out a cynical chuckle. I told Dotti, "I might as well put a new Jeep Grand Cherokee, a mountain cabin in Vail, and a first edition by Faulkner on my list."

"Why do you say that?" she asked.

"Because I have about as much chance of getting those things as some of the ones on my list. What am I thinking? Why bother to even get my hopes up?"

I thought about what my grandmother used to tell me around

Christmas time when I was a boy. She was raised in a Tennessee orphanage, and she said the key to not being disappointed Christmas morning was knowing what to hope for. In other words, don't hope for anything you can't reasonably expect.

Expectations versus Hope

The distinction between what we expect and what we hope for came up in another way. I had lunch with Bob, a friend I once was close with, the kind of friend you want to keep for a lifetime because you've experienced rich moments of soul connection, deep moments of sharing pain, and the joy of worshiping the Father together. However, Bob and I have drifted apart over the last year. We call and see each other less and less, and when we do, we keep it superficial. Occasionally, we have an earnest discussion about our friendship and we both admit we've failed the other and want to re-deepen the friendship. Then we seem to go back to our old ways.

Gradually, after I initiated this conversation a few times, I realized I wanted much more from the friendship than Bob did. At least, I wanted more than he was willing to admit he wanted. When I met Bob for lunch, after a lapse of several noncommunicative months, we had a pleasant meal and caught up on the events of our lives. Neither of us brought up the drift we had experienced. However, when it was time to go, I felt so sad and angry at Bob that I couldn't stand it. He said, "It's great to see you; we'll have to do this again soon."

"It's hard to see you," I replied. "I hate that our friendship has come to this."

He looked me in the eye, knowing instantly what I was talking about. After a couple of minutes, he said, "I'm sorry you didn't get what you expected from our time today."

Without thinking, I said, "Oh, I got what I expected today, just not what I'd hoped for." And then I walked away, got in my car, and left.

I'm certainly not justifying my angry retort; Bob and I both share responsibility for what has happened in our friendship. But my last words to him that day stunned me as much as they stunned him.

Logically, realistically, I knew that Bob and I would not have the kind of conversation or connection I longed for. Based on that objective data, I would have predicted the kind of lunch we had. But I couldn't help wanting more, in part because I'd tasted it before with him, and in a larger part, because relationship is what I'm created for.

It's what you're created for, too. A desire for connection with another is an inherent characteristic of having an eternal soul. In the variety of relationships we experience—with spouses, friends, family, coworkers, acquaintances—we learn to hope for different levels of connection, seeking to transcend our loneliness and separateness from one another.

In the film *Shadowlands*, C. S. Lewis is depicted as being reminded of this valuable lesson by one of his Oxford students. The student's father had taught the boy that we read to be reminded that we are not alone. By the film's end, after Lewis's wife has died of cancer, he states, "We *love* to remind ourselves that we are not alone."

The Voice of Hope

Indeed, this longing for loving connection is nowhere more present than in our prayer lives. Even when we don't feel like praying, or it feels like we're in a spiritual "dry spell" but we obediently go through the motions anyway, we're still expressing something about the way we hope or the way we're afraid to hope for God's presence in our lives. The essence of prayer is the communication of this relational hope to our Father; prayer becomes the voice of our hope.

Since we can't yet fully experience intimacy with Him in the way we long to, we often try to numb this desire to protect ourselves from disappointment and the dull ache of missing Him. But we are called to be people of hope, which is the mystery of our faith, "Christ in you, the *hope* of glory" (Colossians 1:27, emphasis added). In fact, if we examine the roots of the word *hope* from the Hebrew and Greek, we find that it means "request," as well as "wish." We ask (request) God's presence in our lives as well as long (wish) for it.

Prayer, as both a fruit and a root of hope, is an inherent part of our humanity, a reflection of our innate desire to seek and relate to God. In a recent *Life* magazine article (March 1994), over 70 percent of Americans said they pray regularly. Of the folks who said they don't believe in God, about 10 percent of those surveyed said they pray anyway, just in case. This seems to support my belief that in prayer we authentically express our deepest thoughts, feelings, and desires to our Father. We long to know and be known by Him who knows us best. We ache to fully bask in His love and to love Him in return. What keeps us from praying this way?

I believe that the greatest barrier to a fruitful prayer life is not our insecurity about beginning from where we are, nor our busyness. Fear of expressing honest emotions, especially the negative ones, gets closer to it. At the heart of our resistance to prayer is the fear of hope.

In Ecclesiastes 3:11 the scribe writes, "He has made everything beautiful in its time. He has also set eternity in the hearts of men; yet they cannot fathom what God has done from beginning to end." Ken Wilson, with whom I studied the book of Ecclesiastes, stated the theme of the book succinctly when he said that in our earthly condition *we have time on our hands but eternity in our hearts.* Because we are created in the image of the immortal God . . . because He has given us a soul, we hope. We long to seek life, comfort, pleasure, beauty, truth, justice, and everything chocolate. We hope. If we do not, we die. This is chronically true for all of us—it's part of the human condition. However, when Christ dwells in us and the Spirit breathes in our hearts, I believe that hope becomes acute.

Defining Hope

Let me explain further. We often use words like *hope, desire, expect,* and *long* interchangeably. But they don't have the same meaning. *Desire* is pretty basic. It's simply the wish for something—a request, a craving. As I watch my daughter Annie interact with her first few months of life, I realize we all have desire right off the bat. Annie desires milk, sleep, to be held, to be comfortable, to have her diaper changed. We all desire the basics of life and we even learn to make them more sophisticated. And of course, we can pervert our desires and let them rule us.

Expect means "to look forward to," "to anticipate," and is usually based on some prior experience—external data, past experiences, observations. I expect that when I go to church we will sing hymns, we will worship and confess, and someone will speak. Then we'll go home. I have something with which to compare my expectation. It allows me to project, to speculate on what the outcome will actually be.

Hope, on the other hand, combines both desire and expectation. It carries with it the desire or wish for something with the expectation of its fulfillment.

Desire wants something that may or may not be attainable. Desire can be based on need, but often is affected by our emotions and moods. Expectation draws on a basis of comparison. I know what to expect for Thanksgiving dinner because I experience it year after year. As a result of the everyday kinds of expectations I see fulfilled, I learn to hope — to expect things that would please me, be good for me, or suit me. Hope expects. And I believe that biblical hope can be summed up by the word *longing*—a strong, persistent yearning or desire that cannot be entirely fulfilled presently.

Consider all the varieties of hope embodied in a single prayer. This morning I prayed for a friend who is traveling, for inspiration to write this book, for a friend in grief, for the health and spirits of my wife and children. I thanked God for providing for me and my family in some unexpected ways. I thanked Him for life, for the green redbud flourishing outside my window.

As you can see, most of my prayer was self-centered. I asked for many things that would make my life easier, more effective, more comfortable. By asking, I inferred that those things I ask for are possible, despite appearances, probability, logic, or luck. I am hoping. At the same time, I acknowledge that sustaining such hope becomes a struggle when I don't receive answered prayer or experience the kind of warm connection with God I desire. As all of us do, I've hoped for things and been crushed with disappointment when they don't happen.

Last summer a teaching job came open where I teach part-time. Many faculty members encouraged me to apply as a well-qualified and well-liked candidate, and so I did. The application process was long and tedious; the waiting for a decision even more so. I prayed fervently for the job, for the security it would provide (ah, health insurance!) and for the opportunities it would create to interact with students and other faculty. During the wait more faculty members came to me and said, "You're perfect for that job; I know you'll get it." I asked God for this job daily, almost hourly it seemed, for weeks. I tried to maintain faith, to sustain hope that the job and I were meant for each other, but my uneasiness grew, and sure enough, I didn't get the position. I was even informed that it had come down to me and one other candidate, a backhanded consolation.

My angry heart pounded the venom of bitterness throughout my entire being. A half hour after receiving the news, I was scheduled to do an interview about my latest book. I couldn't very well sulk on the radio show like I wanted to; I had to become the gracious interviewee, the writer with deep thoughts and spiritual insights on repentance, of all things. It seemed as if God wouldn't even allow me the downtime I needed to lament my loss.

As self-orbiting as I am, I know there are many deeper, harsher losses. What happens to our prayer lives during such seasons? For me, in the previous example, it meant internalizing my anger and condemning myself as a fool for even hoping that such a thing was possible. This allowed me to get immersed in self-pity and pretend that I had more control over life than I do.

Think for a moment about what makes your heart sick. What have you prayed for and hoped for and prayed for some more? Only your prayer was never answered, or if it was, the answer opposed your request. How did you respond? How did you feel? What kinds of prayers, if any, followed such events?

Hope Deferred

After my pouting and yelling, two thoughts surfaced—a poem by Langston Hughes and Proverbs 13:12: "Hope deferred makes the heart sick, but a longing fulfilled is a tree of life." What does this Scripture mean? How does it relate to my job loss, let alone my hope in Christ?

Eugene Peterson translates the verse this way: "Unrelenting disappointment leaves you heartsick, but a sudden good break can turn life around" (MSG). Why? Because it reminds us of God's goodness and our dependence on Him, regardless how adept we are at controlling, manipulating, denying, or suppressing.

What about the alternative? What can a bad break do for us besides leave us heartsick? How can it drive us back to God?

I don't know if Langston Hughes, poet laureate of the Harlem Renaissance, knew Proverbs 13:12 when he wrote the poem "Harlem" in 1951. I'm betting that he did.

> What happens to a dream deferred?
> Does it dry up
> like a raisin in the sun?
> Or fester like a sore—
> And then run?
> Does it stink like rotten meat?
> Or crust and sugar over—
> Like a syrupy sweet?
>
> Maybe it just sags
> Like a heavy load.
> Or does it explode?[1]

The poem shows keen insight into human nature in all its options. When we defer hope and resign ourselves to "unrelenting disappointment," we can move toward despair, the absence of any hope whatsoever. In Hughes's poem, we see the slow, gradual loss of hope as it shrinks to "a raisin in the sun," a hard, shriveled little shell of what it once was.

Or perhaps hope deferred leaves a festering wound of bitterness if we've made our hope conditional on what we've hoped for. Our anger and disappointment oozes out of us, permeating and poisoning our lives and our approach to the Father.

There's also the rancid smell of evil, the "stink [of] rotten meat," as hope deferred decides to serve itself and take whatever means to fulfill itself. The ultimate disappointment in hope turns to total selfishness and tries to find ways to obtain what God does not seem willing to provide. This is idolatry.

There's also the denial of disappointment implied in the way we "crust and sugar over—/Like a syrupy sweet." Our anger and our longings can get stuffed down inside us as we paint on a happy Christian veneer. This disguise covers up the painful realities of life and seeks to dwell only in forced, superficial "joy."

At the end of the poem, Hughes asks if the dream deferred sags or if it explodes. I believe both are required in the Christian journey of faith. We sometimes sag through the heavy load of our longing to be completely free of our sinful natures and this fallen planet. We suffer now until we can be embraced and welcomed by our Abba Father in heaven. Part of suffering, however, means that we explode—we express the depth of our anger and disappointment at God rather than kill our soul with despair and numbing indifference. Honest explosions keep the lines of communication open and refocus our attention on God, eventually opening us to humility, grace, and faith.

Our prayers give voice to our deepest longings for relationship with God, even amidst the pain, disappointment, and sorrow of this life. Such courageous communication actively hopes beyond the immediate world we see with our eyes and corresponds with the heavenly world we long for with our souls.

Hope's Evil Twin

Hopeful living, despite how simple and natural it is, can easily become subverted to a kind of low-grade fever. We hate disappointment, rejection of any kind, and the onslaught of despair it can lead to. So we often seek to protect ourselves from such pain and avoid it at any cost. We then feel justified in making ourselves the center of things, since we're all we really know and can seemingly control.

Because hopeful living often feels risky, foolish even, we had rather live mediocre lives, rehearsing the motions of life but never living with passionate hope. We disconnect our heart-voiced cries to our Father or we go through the motions, mouthing hollow words to maintain a legal contract. Isn't it ironic that we often choose to live this way—with rage, fear, denial, depression, dis-ease—rather than risk hope?

When we live this way, we're in danger of trying to make God indebted to our service through our legalism, dogmatism, merit systems, and penance. In a very literal sense we want Him in our lives to the extent that He will serve us, like an excellent waiter with the powers of Aladdin's genie, but not so that we can have a passionate relationship with Him as His child and know His personality and, ultimately, His will for us.

We offer Him our acts of passionless prayer or service or legalistic Bible study and quiet times, then demand that He come through for us the way we want Him to. When He doesn't, we think, *He must not love us, He must not be good, He must not care about us or He would do what we want.* We lose perspective of His Godhood, of His holiness, His power and omniscience. In our age of the info-superhighway, of "microwave" service in every facet of our society, we often perceive God as the ultimate foolproof software package at our fingertips. And when the program doesn't run to our satisfaction, we shut down our hope and withdraw communication.

In retaliation for our disappointment, we look outside of God for something to nourish our spirits, something to fulfill us. But the objects of those desires and the extremes we carry them to are incapable of meeting the heart's deepest longing. Whether we call them addictions or conditional pleasures, we run from new product to new management system, looking for life abundant.

Often what we turn to may be good in itself, in moderation, context, and perspective, but we take it to the extreme and idolize it. Exercise is good, sexuality is good, wanting to be comfortable is good, but we make our life's fulfillment contingent on possessing the desired object and then discover it cannot satisfy us. So we discard what we desire like a banana peel and rarely learn anything from our dissatisfaction because we're on to the next banana in another far-off tree. We tease ourselves with the fickleness of our hearts and the selfishness of our desires. We resist embracing the true appetite of our souls, our hunger for relationship with our Abba Father. Instead, we focus on the "unrelenting" disappointment that comes with life. And we kill our hope.

Hope Does Not Disappoint

Scripture often portrays the fickleness of the human heart. One of the most obvious examples is the ongoing theme of the nation of Israel's wishy-washy heart toward Yahweh. One moment the Israelites worship with sincere fervor and a passion for obedience, and the next they pass the hat to collect enough gold to create a tangible object of worship.

In Hosea, Israel is compared to a harlot who forsakes the deep, abiding love of a faithful and good man for the forbidden pleasure of a ten-minute tryst.

In Jeremiah the people are compared to broken cisterns that continually try to mend themselves and quench their own thirst without success (2:13).

In Isaiah 50:10-11 they are compared to night travelers continually trying to light their own paths with the shallow spark of their self-idolatry.

God, on the other hand, is tireless and faithful. Beyond any reasonable explanation, the nature of His grace is that *He never gives up on us.* He consistently offers forgiveness, mercy, new beginnings, and water cold and deep from the well of His Being.

The Father speaks through the prophet Isaiah:

> Come, all you who are thirsty,
>   come to the waters;
> and you who have no money,
>   come, buy and eat!
> Come, buy wine and milk
>   without money and without cost.
> Why spend money on what is not
>   bread,
>   and your labor on what does not
>   satisfy?
> Listen, listen to me, and eat what is
>   good,
>   and your soul will delight in the
>   richest of fare. (55:1-2)

Today I think the prophet might say, "Why do you hope in things you know can't fulfill you? Why do you tantalize yourself?"

Why do we find it so hard to access the hope that transcends the disappointments life throws at us? It's because we have to endure the disappointments and the unfulfilled desires. Endurance means living in the present, even when it's painful, and trusting God that the pain or discomfort is for our *ultimate* good, not what we perceive as our *immediate* good. The apostle Paul describes this mindset:

We also rejoice in our sufferings, because we know that suffering produces perseverance; perseverance, character; and character, hope. And hope does not disappoint us, because God has poured out his love into our hearts by the Holy Spirit, whom he has given us. (Romans 5:3-5)

We have to embrace the tension of waiting for the fulfillment of what we already have. Prayer forces us to patiently wait and continually communicate with God through all the anger, craziness, and self-absorption. Prayer forces us to hope, even if most of what we hope for seems obscure and small, or even impossible. Prayer forces us to at least recall our hope that God hears us and listens and cares.

For now, we're required to wait for the ultimate consummation of our love affair with God, to wait patiently until we can bask in His presence forever. In the meantime, our Father asks us to draw near to Him as we experience the fullness of life's unrelenting disappointments. He wants us to live by hope — the sparks of desire that serve as signal flares of heaven.

Hope is a miracle, every bit as mysterious as the Trinity, as the Resurrection, as turning water into wine or feeding thousands of people from a little bread and fish. Hope is the gift of Christ, the essence of the gospel, the faith as small as a mustard seed. It's the fuel of an alive, grace-tasting, faith-acting soul.

Hope is the essence of prayer; prayer is the embodiment of hope.

The Moon Is Round

I can think of many examples that embody prayerful hope, but one in particular continues to resonate. Recently, our fourteen-year-old niece ended her battle with leukemia. Her family and friends, and thousands of people lifted up prayers for her healing, beseeching a gracious God to restore her body, to restore her life. Frequently I found myself on my knees in my office or teary-eyed driving down the highway. After more than a year-long battle, she died anyway.

Two memories echo in my mind. The first occurred immediately after she died. At the hospital, my brother-in-law found himself trying to console and dismiss the hundred or so people who had gathered that night. He prayed in their midst; and not just a "I-don't-know-what-else-to-do" prayer but a heart cry, a lament for our loss of Christy and a praise for her gain into heaven. He prayed, "If we ask why, Father, don't let us stop there. Let us get up in the morning and love You again."

That kind of prayer was honest and plainspoken, true to the bone of the anger, doubt, loss, and odd joy we all felt. It was a prayer that acknowledged where so many of us were that night, yet it still pointed us toward hope.

I also recall the graveside service. The pastor delivered a warm, hopeful eulogy, describing Christy's enormous impact in such a short time. He talked about her faith, her hope even in the midst of excruciating pain and debilitating disease. As evidence, he read from a small pocket notebook in which Christy had recorded her favorite verses. He read verse after verse and then paused awkwardly. "I'm not sure what this is," he said. "I don't think it's a verse I know. It says, 'The moon is round.'" He smiled and kept going.

Later, Christy's mom explained the story behind that verse. Christy had made friends with another young leukemia victim who told her that God was bigger than their disease. "If you have trouble remembering that, or if it doesn't feel like it, just look up at the moon," the friend had told Christy. "We only see part of it at a time—half-moon, quarter-moon. Even when it's a full moon, it's only two-dimensional. We never can see the whole roundness of the moon from where we look on earth. The moon is round."

Those words have become a prayer of mine. In desperate moments, I simply whisper, "The moon is round," and I remember a little girl wasting away yet praying a hope that is bigger than her death or my doubt, lost jobs, or overdue bills.

Revolutionary Patience

One of my favorite writers, Anne Lamott, heard a preacher define hope the same way she defines writing: "revolutionary patience." A wise, process-oriented writer and teacher herself, Lamott stresses to students that it's the sustained journey of writing that makes better writers. Similarly, it's the sustained process of hoping and expressing that hope through the day-to-day conversation of prayer that makes us stronger

Christians. Such a commitment to communicate with God throughout our journey (not just the good times or the needy moments) produces a richer intimacy with our Father. The relationship between our hope and our willingness to pray becomes symbiotic: Prayer produces more willingness to hope, to be in touch with our desire for connection with God, and hope produces a greater longing to commune with Him.

The Psalms always conclude with this hope, with the revolutionary patience to wait on God, to trust that He's up to good, even when we suffer:

> *I waited patiently* for the LORD;
>   he turned to me and heard my cry.
> He lifted me out of the slimy pit,
>   out of the mud and mire;
> he set my feet on a rock
>   and gave me a firm place to stand.
> He put a new song in my mouth,
>   a hymn of praise to our God. (Psalm 40:1-3, emphasis added)

This kind of patient hope undermines the despair that arises out of our shortsighted and painful awareness of the present:

> I would have despaired unless I had believed that I
>   would see the goodness of the LORD
> In the land of the living.
> Wait for the LORD;
> Be strong, and let your heart take courage;
> Yes, wait for the LORD. (Psalm 27:13-14, NASB)

Our Father sustains us with a supernatural hope that transcends our limited imaginations. This hope can consistently draw us back to communicating with Him if we'll let it.

Yes, waiting and hoping is not easy, but they are an inherent part of growing up spiritually. They are the growing pains of a new creation being forged within us by a loving Father.

When we pray, we affirm and actualize the living hope that is our love and salvation through, from, and of Jesus Christ, His Father, and His Spirit. Prayer is the vehicle of hope in the midst of an often hope-less-*appearing* world. As we learn that praying without ceasing is eas-ier than we think, we experience a hope that transcends fear and grows in love.

Questions for Prayer and Reflection

1. What kinds of things do you hope for on a day-to-day basis? What things do you keep yourself from hoping? Why?

2. How do you define the word *hope?* What's the difference between hoping for a new car and hoping in Christ? Do the two intersect in any way?

3. What is the hardest part about hope for you? In other words, what does it cost you to hope?

4. Describe the relationship between what you hope in and how you pray. Are the two interrelated in your life? Why or why not?

5. How do you sustain your hope when terrible events—like death, divorce, or illness—strike? What is necessary for you to continue to pray through these times?

My Lord God,
give me once more the courage to hope;
merciful God,
let me hope once again,
fructify my barren and infertile mind.[2]

—SÖREN KIERKEGAARD

PART TWO

THE PRAYER-CENTERED LIFE: CHANNELS OF PRAYER

—

*Every time you pray, if your prayer is sincere,
there will be new feeling and new meaning in it
which will give you fresh courage, and you will understand
that prayer is an education.*

—DOSTOEVSKI, BROTHERS KARAMAZOV

—

*Prayer is not eloquence, but earnestness;
not the definition of helplessness, but the feeling of it;
not figures of speech, but earnestness of soul.*

—HANNAH MORE

—

Lord, teach us to pray.

—LUKE 11:1

FINDING
OUR VOICE

*Prayer does not change God,
but changes him who prays.*[1]
—SÖREN KIERKEGAARD

W hen I teach creative writing classes, it's easy to discern some students' favorite writers. Most student writers tend to imitate, and I usually end up with a couple of Stephen Kings, a Jane Austen or two, a budding Hemingway, a Danielle Steele fan, and several Tolkiens.

Imitation may indeed be the highest form of flattery, but the goal in writing is to discover one's unique writing style, one's own voice. I don't discourage students from imitating—it's often how they learn best—but I do encourage them not to emulate any one author. They need to discover their own strengths and weaknesses and how to use them, because no one else can write just like they can.

In a similar way, no one can pray just like you. Each of us plays a unique and remarkable role in a vast relational network. What we do, how we live, what we say has a powerful impact on the people around us. While it's not a revelation that we affect those around us, we're often unaware of exactly how we can set in motion a whole chain of influence we may never see in a tangible way.

Do you recall Jimmy Stewart's character, George Bailey, in *It's a Won-*

derful Life? George learns the hard way that every life is unique and pur-
poseful. This valuable lesson is true for all of us. We must remember
that our prayers directly and indirectly affect the world around us.

Although we have a tremendous influence on others, it is ourselves
that we affect most through prayer. The longer we spend abiding in
God's presence, the better we'll know Him and the deeper our love will
grow for Him. As our relationship with our Father deepens, we discover
more of our prayer "voice." We lose ourselves in our Father's presence
and discover more of who we truly are. Jesus reminds us of this paradox: "For whoever wants to save his life will lose it; but whoever loses
his life for me will find it" (Matthew 16:25).

The Sighs of Life

You don't need to acquire a skill to find your voice. It's who you are; it's
simply you sharing with your Abba Father in honesty and hope. In fact,
whether or not you consider it prayer, your life already "speaks" your
attitude about your relationship with God. You're probably already
doing more praying than you realize just by the way you live your life
in response to Him.

If you're ignoring Him, or only going through the motions of
what you think He wants from you, you're sending a message as loud
and clear as if you took a bullhorn and raised it to the sky and yelled,
"Since we're not communicating on my terms, then I don't have much
to say to You." Or recall those moments when your heart flooded with
joy and your praise and gratitude to God transcended words. Those
times force us to extend our understanding of prayer beyond the
words we sometimes mouth from a devotional guide.

Consider how writer Frederick Buechner defines this relational
view of prayer:

> Everybody prays whether he thinks of it as praying or not.
> The odd silence you fall into when something very beautiful is
> happening or something very good or very bad. The ah-h-h!
> that sometimes floats up out of you as out of a Fourth of July
> crowd when the sky-rocket bursts over the water. The stam-
> mer of pain at somebody else's pain. The stammer of joy

at somebody else's joy. Whatever words or sounds you use for sighing with over your own life. These are all prayers in their own way. These are all spoken not just to yourself but to something even more familiar than yourself and even more strange than the world.[2]

Perhaps Buechner's way of describing prayer makes you uncomfortable, or perhaps it seems as natural as daydreaming. Either way, consider what you're saying to God most days as you release a deep sigh, either out of joy or sorrow, repulsion or affection. What stirs in you as you read the morning headline about the drive-by shooting? What's your reaction when you see a toddler tackle an ice-cream cone on a warm spring day? What do you long to say to your friend who's going through a divorce? To your spouse about your desire to be closer? Can these be prayers?

Opening Up to God

Our honest responses to the world around us are the catalyst for a prayer-centered life. I use the word *catalyst* because *where* we direct our responses ultimately determines whether or not our honest responses become prayers. We can choose to brood over the painful circumstances of life, worrying and fretting about how we'll pay our bills or wishing our family's health was something we could control. Such ownership directs our responses inward so that we pridefully attempt to take responsibility for the circumstances of life. Or we might direct our responses outward but not upward; we make someone else or some other event conditionally responsible for our peace and well-being.

If we go in either of these directions, we set ourselves up for disappointment. When we cling to our own abilities, trying new strategies and different techniques to make life run smoother, easier, and more comfortably, we're unlikely to turn toward our Father in humble acknowledgment of our dependence on Him. When we try to control things, our reluctance to pray increases, because it's difficult to maintain the facade of control when we're on our knees.

In his rich and simple book on prayer, *With Open Hands,* Henri Nouwen explains:

The resistance to praying is like the resistance of tightly clenched fists. This image shows a tension, a desire to cling tightly to yourself, a greediness which betrays fear. A story about an elderly woman brought to a psychiatric center exemplifies this attitude. She was wild, swinging at everything in sight, and frightening everyone so much that the doctors had to take everything away from her. But there was one small coin which she gripped in her fist and would not give up. In fact, it took two people to pry open that clenched hand. It was as though she would lose her very self along with the coin. If they deprived her of that last possession, she would have nothing more and be nothing more. That was her fear.

When you are invited to pray, you are asked to open your tightly clenched fists and give up your last coin. But who wants to do that? . . . You feel it safer to cling to a sorry past than to trust in a new future. So you fill your hands with small, clammy coins which you don't want to surrender.[3]

Our honest responses to life are invitations to pray. If we don't clench our fists around the coins of self-control, then we'll find ourselves offering our worries to Him who cares even about the death of a sparrow (Matthew 10:29).

When we feel the self-imposed confines of worry and fear, we can supersede these feelings with love, hope, and faith. The sighs of life can lead us either to despair, as we realize how desperately we fail at making life work like we want it to, or upward to our Father's embrace. This relational approach to prayer will cause us to view prayer as a natural part of our everyday life.

In his instruction on Christian conduct to the Thessalonians, Paul charges Christians to "pray continually" (1 Thessalonians 5:17). When we view prayer as a skill to be acquired and developed, Paul's exhortation feels impossibly exhausting. He might as well tell us to juggle oranges without ceasing. Instead, he reminds us to do something as inherently natural in the spiritual life as breathing.

Rather than dread Paul's challenge, we can rejoice in the intimacy afforded by such accessibility to our Father. We don't have to wait until our busyness subsides or until we feel especially close to God. Instead, we invite our Father's presence into every aspect of our busy, sometimes tedious days.

Practicing God's Presence

I was first exposed to this method of prayer when I read Brother Lawrence's *The Practice of the Presence of God*, a collection of his letters and conversations put together after his death by his abbot, Joseph de Beaufort. I was struck with the singular beauty, clarity, and simplicity of such a concept. It revolutionized my prayer life by allowing me to be who I am in the moment of my daily circumstances and still seek God. I could invite Him into my life as I drove to work, taught class, ate lunch, visited with friends.

Brother Lawrence's view of prayer also removed the pressure I felt to conform my prayer life to what I saw in other Christians and what I read in various books and heard in assorted sermons. I learned to seek God throughout the day and to cultivate communication like I would in a friendship.

Who was this saint who left such a spiritual legacy? Brother Lawrence grew up as Nicholas Herman in a poor family in a small town in France in the seventeenth century. After living as a soldier and footman, Herman joined a lay community of Carmelites in Paris and was assigned to the kitchen. For the next twenty-five years until his death, Brother Lawrence lived a rather mundane exterior life of cleaning pots and pans. Yet his spiritual life grew like a giant as he discovered how to incorporate prayer into all aspects of his day. Frustrated with the variety of techniques and formalities that he heard and read about, Brother Lawrence determined to "give my all for God's all."[4]

It wasn't easy at first. Like us, Brother Lawrence found his mind drifting, his discipline lacking, and his guilt and anger growing at his lack of focus. But he discovered that he could move beyond those emotional barriers, persevere despite those feelings, to cultivate God's presence on a daily, even hourly, basis until it became more natural and habitual. While his perseverance may sound like obligation, it's clear from his writings that he was motivated by his loving commitment to know the Father. In fact, he reached a turning point just as he was about to quit. By letting go of his controlling attempts to force himself to converse with God and feel God's presence in response, he discovered a sense of peace, a place of being who he was in the moment and going from there. He discovered what it means to live life with God at your side moment by moment.

That meant that Brother Lawrence found himself experiencing God while scrubbing dirty pots in "an habitual, silent, and secret conversation. I keep myself by a simple attention and a general fond regard to God, which I refer to as an *actual presence* of God."[5]

By abandoning all the formulas of his day, and pursuing God on a continual, moment-by-moment basis, Brother Lawrence grew in faith, love, and intimacy with his Father.

Consider how true and revolutionary this remains today. We live the Christian faith in the trenches at the office, where we try to keep our cool even as our boss makes unreasonable demands; in the home, as we seek to remain patient and loving with our children when they're scribbling on the walls with crayons. How about when we're stuck in a traffic jam, or stuck behind a fast-food counter, or thousands of other places where we live out the unglamorous substance of our lives?

The walk of faith is not for Sunday or for the once-a-year spiritual retreat. The life of prayer is not for when you get your act together and finally start showing up on time to check in with God. Faith and prayer are nothing if not practical. They are the essence of what we do, how we act, who we are, who we're becoming, where we come from, and where we're going.[6]

Everyday Use

What keeps my prayer life alive, other than God's Spirit in me, is my desire to experience God every day, even as I teach classes, grade papers, prepare lessons, write books, wash dishes, play with my girls, love my wife.

During my thirty-minute commute to work, I often find myself turning off the radio (for I love the clatter of voices), gazing up at the skyline, and basking in my Father's presence. I reflect on my actions, words, and motivations that reveal selfishness, and hurt my relationship with my Father. I embrace His forgiveness and move on to voice my worries and concerns about what's ahead. I ask for His guidance and strength and wisdom. I simply bask in His quiet.

In the classroom, I catch a moment while the class completes a writing assignment and I remember my Father, remember that I'm not nearly as alone or harried or frazzled as I feel. I have the One who loves me most right there with me. It's how I survive the busiest of days and seasons. It's how I survive the slowest and most relaxing of days as well. It's part of what relationship means to me—consistent two-way communication.

The sharp contrast between relational prayer, which practices the presence of God on a daily basis, and obligational prayer, which goes through the motions and leaves you feeling guilty when you don't do it, reminds me of Alice Walker's fine short story, "Everyday Use." A hard-working, uneducated, but shrewd country woman, Mrs. Johnson has always found it difficult to say no to her grown daughter Dee. A free-spirited, successful woman of the world, Dee has built a life for herself by sheer will and determination. As the story begins she is returning home with her boyfriend to get in touch with her rural roots. Dee's sister, Maggie, is the antithesis of the polished, suave sophisticate. Maggie is shy, scarred from a fire, and used to being a passive victim, bound up in her life in the Georgia countryside.

Dee decides that she wants to take several household objects—a butter churn, a quilt—back to the city with her as "objets d'art." Mama consents to everything except the quilt, which has already been promised to Maggie as part of her dowry. This sets off a fierce exchange:

> "Maggie can't appreciate these quilts!" she [Dee] said, "She'd probably be backward enough to put them to everyday use."
>
> "I reckon she would," I [Mama] said. "God knows I been saving 'em for long enough with nobody using 'em. I hope she will."
>
> "But they're priceless!" she was saying now, furiously; for she has a temper. "Maggie would put them on the bed and in five years they'd be in rags. Less than that!"
>
> "She can always make some more," I said. "Maggie knows how to quilt."[7]

This exchange, along with the rest of the story, enforces a theme of living out one's legacy on a daily basis rather than simply referring to it historically and hanging souvenirs on the wall: Dee would hang the quilt as a museum piece, but Maggie would use it daily because she knows how to quilt, to sustain the legacy. While the story pertains to our ancestral heritage, it also has implications for our spiritual heritage, for the way we live out our faith, for the way we seek to know God through prayer. We are called to make our Father the relational priority of our lives—every day.

Bed and Breakfast with God

Maybe some of you are squirming right now. You're saying, "That pray-as-you-go-along stuff is fine, and I've tried it, but I never really connect with God unless I set apart a block of time and free my mind of distractions and focus intently on Him."

That's understandable. In fact, for my friends who ask me how to pray when they're too busy, I remind them of Brother Lawrence. At the same time, I know there are individual differences of need and desire in our prayer lives. In addition to being called to live our lives within the presence of God, we are also called to set apart time for Him and Him alone.

Most of us would agree that we make time for the people who are most important to us. When a stranger calls my office with a request, I do my best to call him or her back when I can. When a colleague or friend calls, I return the call as soon as I'm free. But when my wife calls, I will drop everything to talk with her. Even so, there are times when my wife and I simply need to be alone together in order for us to reconnect, to deepen and grow in our marriage.

One of our favorite ways to get away together is to head for the mountains and a favorite bed and breakfast inn. The intimacy of someone's home, along with the cozy warmth of homemade food and breathtaking views inspires us to draw closer together, to share our feelings and struggles.

I try to view time alone with my Father in the same way. Sometimes we need to get away from our normal routines to seek Him. Numerous biblical examples reinforce this. The prophet Elijah experiences

God's provision during a drought as he hears the Lord instructing him, "Leave here, turn eastward and hide in the Kerith Ravine, east of the Jordan. You will drink from the brook, and I have ordered the ravens to feed you there" (1 Kings 17:3-4). Elijah's example reminds us, perhaps metaphorically, that our Father often nourishes us even amidst the droughts of our busy, troubled lives, if we let Him.

Jesus encounters a similar refreshment in His consistent pursuit of the Father. Relational communication is clearly the cornerstone of His entire life and ministry. Even in the hustle and bustle of fame and notoriety, Jesus consistently seeks out quiet moments and lonely places to commune with God. "Very early in the morning, while it was still dark, Jesus got up, left the house and went off to a solitary place, where he prayed" (Mark 1:35). Prior to full public disclosure of Jesus' ministry, "[He] often withdrew to lonely places and prayed" (Luke 5:16).

Whether you actually go to a bed and breakfast or simply carve out time in your favorite chair at home, try to imagine pursuing this kind of intimacy with your Father. Such times bring refreshment and renewal, but they also may require that you enter the dry, lonely places within you as you cry out to Him from the depths of your being.

Alone in the Desert

While Jesus' retreats with the Father nourished Him, we must also notice that they often forced the Son to confront temptation, fear, grief, and uncertainty. We first notice this kind of set-apart intimacy sandwiched between Jesus' baptism and the beginning of His public ministry.

In Matthew 4, Jesus is "led by the Spirit into the desert to be tempted by the devil. After fasting forty days and forty nights, he was hungry." (verses 1-2). While it's debatable, the heart of this retreat focuses around Jesus' being tempted, around His rebuking Satan and rising above the very real temptations of food, self-identity, and power.[8] There's a sense of intimate preparation on Jesus' part for the upcoming temptation He'll endure.

In the desert, a barren place free of distractions, He likely felt the abiding intimacy He inherently recalled experiencing in heaven as part of the Trinity, as the Beloved Son. The fact that He knew who He was—more than just His physical hunger—and that He didn't have to prove anything about His deity or whether God loved Him freed Him up to remember His dependence on His Abba.

As we see from Jesus' confrontation with the devil, these times of retreat are not necessarily comfortable. If we consider Christ's time in the Garden of Gethsemane prior to His death, we see an even more barren aloneness.

> Then Jesus went with them to a garden called Gethsemane and told his disciples, "Stay here while I go over there and pray." Taking along Peter and the two sons of Zebedee, he plunged into an agonizing sorrow. Then he said, "This sorrow is crushing my life out. Stay here and keep vigil with me."
>
> Going a little ahead, he fell on his face, praying, "My Father, if there is any way, get me out of this. But please, not what I want. You, what do *you* want?"
>
> When he came back to his disciples, he found them sound asleep. He said to Peter, "Can't you stick it out with me a single hour? Stay alert; be in prayer so you don't wander into temptation without even knowing you're in danger. . . ."
>
> He then left them a second time. Again he prayed, "My Father, if there is no other way than this, drinking this cup to the dregs, I'm ready. Do it your way."
>
> When he came back, he again found them sound asleep. They simply couldn't keep their eyes open. This time he let them sleep on, and went back a third time to pray, going over the same ground one last time. (Matthew 26:36-44, MSG)

Notice the deep emotion and soul-wrenching loneliness Jesus experiences as He seeks communion with His Father at the most crucial juncture of His life. While He longs for His friends to keep watch, to join Him in His endeavor, Jesus also knows that He must be alone for this divine conversation. As part of His sacrifice for us, Jesus was willing to seek His Father's divine will even in the midst of being fully human—scared perhaps, saddened, angry at His friends, about to be betrayed by one of His own. He seeks God anyway. He enters into this desert of spirit and seeks His Father's face.

We not only have to pull away physically from our daily routines and go away with God, we have to enter, spiritually and emotionally, our internal deserts and meet God in the midst of our loneliness, depression, and desperation. These are the times when we often least feel like praying.

When I go away for a retreat weekend, I work hard to remove distractions and then find myself alone with God in a small, claustrophobic prayer chapel, in a great expanse of wood, in a quiet room with no one to talk to but Him. And it feels like we're strangers, like I'm an awkward teenager on a first date. I don't like that empty feeling, that "Okay, God, I'm here—now where are You?" I much prefer to think that my effort will be rewarded with a resounding time of joy and spiritual exchange with my Father.

Nonetheless, I believe these desert experiences, these times of internal and external retreat, are just as valuable and necessary as the times when we glimpse the glory of His heaven. I'm much more likely to meet God by embracing my loneliness, my fears and anxieties, than by trying to run away from them and pretend that He's taken them all away. Facing our internal deserts may deepen our longing and loneliness to the point where we feel abandoned by God. This experience is what the mystics, like Saint John of the Cross, often called the "dark night of the soul." But so often, that loneliness is rewarded with an odd closeness with the Father. We learn to live with our longing, to enter into the dim twilight tension of our present faith rather than flee to the darkness of despair or the artificial lights of self-idolatry.

When we face our dark nights, Saint John of the Cross explains, God often purifies us; our longings for His presence become intensified to the point where our selfish desires fall to the wayside. Such an experience uncovers the voice of true longing for our Father, stripping away the many distractions and selfish diversions that occupy our lives. This process is not easy or comfortable, and it requires suffering God's absence in order to love Him more fully. Like Jacob wrestling the angel, we wrestle through barriers to a deeper faith and are eventually blessed by God's presence.

At some point we will all face such a time of walking in the desert, of being alone with the silence of God. Perhaps we will face several of these times. Regardless of frequency, we must stay in touch with our longing for God's presence and our hope in His goodness in order to persevere and grow in faith and intimacy with Him.

Questions for Prayer and Reflection

To find and exercise our voice of prayer requires that we invite God's presence into every aspect of our daily lives as well as seek out moments of aloneness with Him. In many ways this only scratches the surface of what it means to communicate with God and abide in His presence. I encourage you to write and pray your way through the following thoughts and questions.

1. What does it mean for you to rekindle your prayer life from where you are right now, not from where you'd like to be?

2. Annie Dillard writes, "You do not have to sit outside in the dark. If, however, you want to look at the stars, you will find that darkness is required. The stars neither require it nor demand it."[9] What do you suppose she means? How does it relate to your personal pursuit of God through prayer?

3. Imagine yourself alone with God in a quiet room. Without thinking about it or censoring it, describe how you'd feel—terrified, anxious, ecstatic, self-conscious, relieved, furious, awed. Consider what keeps you from honestly pursuing silence with God.

4. What would it mean for you to incorporate more prayer directly into your everyday life? How do you interpret Brother Lawrence's secret to practicing the presence of God wherever you are?

5. Describe your response to Buechner's definition of prayer, "sighing" over one's life. Do you agree with me that such sighing is the beginning of all personal prayers, whether we're aware of it or not? Why or why not?

6. In her collection of poems, *The Weather of the Heart,* Madeleine L'Engle includes this poem:

I, who live by words, am wordless when
I try my words in prayer. All language turns
To silence. Prayer will take my words and then
Reveal their emptiness. The stilled voice learns
To hold its peace, to listen with the heart
To silence that is joy, is adoration.
The self is shattered, all words torn apart
In this strange patterned time of contemplation
That, in time, breaks time, breaks words, breaks me,
And then, in silence, leaves me healed and mended.
I leave, returned to language, for I see
Through words, even when all words are ended.
I, who live by words, am wordless when
I turn me to the Word to pray. Amen.[10]

What does it mean for you to pray without words? How do you interpret this poem? Try writing your own poem that captures what it's like
for you to face the silent place of being alone with the company of God.

*O my God, when will silence, retirement, and prayer become
the occupations of my soul as they are now
frequently the objects of my desires? How am I wearied with
saying so much and yet doing so little for You!
Come, Jesus, come, You the only object of my love,
the center and supreme happiness of my soul!
Come, and impress my mind with such a lively conviction of
Thy presence that all within me may yield
to its influence. Amen.*[11]

—THOMAS À KEMPIS

OPERATING INSTRUCTIONS

*[Jesus] said to them,
"When you pray, say:
'Father, hallowed be your name. . . .'"*
—LUKE 11:2

During fourth grade at my small Catholic school, I brought home a set of rosary beads given to me as a gift. My grandmother was quite alarmed and worried that I was praying "unsuitably." I asked her what she meant, to which she replied, "Jesus makes it very clear that we're not supposed to pray prayers out of rote repetition. That's basically what those beads are for—to count how many times you've recited the same prayers."

"What about the Lord's Prayer?" I asked. "We say it the same way every time we say it in our church, and we're Baptists. How are we supposed to pray then?"

I had her there. She tried to explain, but struggled to distinguish between rote repetition and liturgical prayer with a set form that has a historical and traditional depth to it. Even today, my fourth grade question—How should we pray?—remains an elusive query.

How Should We Pray?

The disciples were no different than we are today. They posed the same question to Jesus. Luke records, "One day Jesus was praying in a certain place. When he finished, one of his disciples said to him, 'Lord, teach us to pray, just as John taught his disciples'" (Luke 11:1). The reference to John's method makes me wonder if the disciple's motive might have been to find a new prayer technique. Nevertheless, Jesus responds with our greatest example of how we should communicate with our Father:

> "When you pray, say,
> 'Father,
> Reveal who you are.
> Set the world right.
> Keep us alive with three square meals.
> Keep us forgiven with you and forgiving others.
> Keep us safe from ourselves and the Devil.'"
> (Luke 11:2-4, MSG)

Jesus' instructions on prayer contain two consistent themes: Pray spontaneously and deliberately—that is, with persistence and without ceasing. In many ways these themes broke in content and form with what His Jewish listeners were used to. Jesus declared that instead of praying only at set times in the synagogue, instead of using the words of their ancestors and prophets, people could now talk directly with Yahweh, the Lord of All, the Feared One. They could call Him *Daddy*.

Imagine that you have a distant business relationship with the CEO of a Japanese conglomerate corporation worth billions of dollars. Let's say you bought a radio or cassette player of theirs, something small, and you wanted to discuss it with the company. You want to tell them what you liked and didn't like about it. You follow the protocol and write straightforward business letters based on what others have written before you, going through the chain of command from person to person. In response the CEO shows up on your doorstep, shakes your hand, and says, "Call me friend. We have a relationship that is so much more than what you're used to. You're not just a nameless customer. I care deeply about you."

My analogy breaks down because God is much, much more than

a CEO. Nonetheless, the message and example Jesus brought to all of us is that we now have direct access with God. He gives us a model and follows up with the closest how-to instruction we can expect. The only operating instructions we need for prayer are contained in the simplicity and beauty of our Lord's prayer. Like a master poet, Jesus includes so much content in such concise language. What does His content teach us about how to pray?

First, we are to address the Father personally and to ask for a revelation of His presence. I think of the word *epiphany* here, a term originally used to describe the visit of the Eastern Magi to the newborn baby Jesus. The word is from the Greek *epiphaneia,* meaning "to manifest or appear." The word has come to mean any sudden revelation, often divine. Thanks to writers like James Joyce,[1] it might very well be a personal realization. In a real sense, an epiphany is what we're asking for when we pray: "Father, reveal Your character to me, let me know You. Let me experience Your presence even as I go to work and eat lunch and drive to the dentist and clean the bathroom."

After asking for God's presence, we pray for global concerns. "Set the world right," as Peterson translates (MSG). "Your kingdom come, your will be done on earth as it is in heaven" (Matthew 6:10). Contained in these few words is a plea for restoration, for redemption, for order, justice, mercy, beauty, and all that is His goodness. As Julian of Norwich wrote, "It behoved that there should be sin; but all shall be well, and all shall be well, and all manner of thing shall be well."[2]

"Your kingdom come" implicitly carries the cry "Maranatha!" It echoes with our hunger and thirst for righteousness (Matthew 5:6), it resonates with our thirst for living water (John 4:10). Once again, Jesus' model of prayer directs us back to our longing for God, our eternal appetite for heaven.

Daily Wonder Bread

Next, the prayer addresses more immediate, personal requests: "Give us today our daily bread" (Matthew 6:11). For Jesus' original audience, these words would immediately conjure the image of the children of Israel wandering in the desert hungry, thirsty, soul-weary. And then the strange sight of a white breadlike substance—manna—falling from the sky.

When I was a child, my Sunday school teacher encouraged me to imagine slices of Wonder Bread falling like leaves from a tree. The Lord provided for His people in the midst of nothing. In a desert where nothing grew or lived, He miraculously delivered bread bakery fresh.

Even though this section of the prayer is a request for food for our bodies, most commentators agree that it symbolizes the entire gamut of small, even trivial, requests. Jesus seems to be giving us permission to bring our most mundane concerns to the center of the universe, God's throne. At first, Jesus' request reminds us of our human frailty. But it's more than just a peanut butter sandwich or a pot roast. It's an invitation to be human. It tells us it's okay to ask for schedules to work out, for friends to love, for work to get done.

Richard Foster explains, "Try to imagine what our prayer experience would be like if he [Jesus] had forbidden us to ask for the little things. What if the only things we were allowed to talk about were the weighty matters, the important things, the profound issues? We would be orphaned in the cosmos, cold, and terribly alone. But the opposite is true: he welcomes us with our 1,001 trifles, for they are each important to him."[3]

Accepting Grace, Avoiding Evil

The prayer then moves from the request for giving to forgiving: "Keep us forgiven with you and forgiving others" (Matthew 6:12, MSG). An inherent part of relationship with God, of course, is forgiveness, both receiving it and extending it. By acknowledging the selfishness that separates us from God, we know we have nothing to make us worthy of God's favor. But ah, there's the rub. The beauty of God's gift, the most selfless thing that anyone could do, He did. Christ died so that we might live. And as the old saying goes, "Salvation is free, but it isn't cheap." The price is usually relinquishment of our pride, being willing—like the prodigal sons and daughters we are—to come home, despite our betrayal, and seek our Father's forgiveness. And He runs out to greet us with a fervent hug that squeezes out all the doubts and fears and shame we had about coming home. And He loves us still more than we could ever imagine.

We'll discuss forgiveness in more depth in the chapter on True

Confession, but for now consider letting go of your pride, shame, guilt, anger, and fear. Embrace the forgiveness He gives. Forgive the persons who have hurt you, failed you, grieved you. The relationship between being forgiven by God and forgiving others is not conditional—that is, God won't withhold forgiveness unless we forgive others. That wouldn't exactly be grace, now would it? But I believe it's a more proportional corollary. We are only *able* to forgive others to the extent that we're willing to embrace God's forgiveness of us.

"And lead us not into temptation, but deliver us from the evil one" (Matthew 6:13). Or, as Peterson puts it, "Keep us safe from ourselves and the Devil" (MSG). When we ask God not to lead us into temptation, are we implying that He does lead us, or could lead us, into temptation? Much debate swirls around this question. I believe that God does not cause us to sin, but He does allow us to face our weaknesses. We can't ignore how Matthew 4:1-11 begins: "Then Jesus was led by the Spirit into the desert to be tempted by the devil." Why in the world would the Spirit lead Jesus to be tempted? Why would God allow Job to be tested? I believe He allows it so we can be reminded of our dependency on Him, of our inherent weaknesses. Temptations provide us with opportunities for worship. We can either give in to sin and bend to the idol of self-gratification, or we can run to our Father for cover.

We should also keep in mind two things about temptation. One, it is a natural by-product of our free will. If there was nothing to choose but God, then we would basically be programmed bodies, something like human pets, without a choice or without sacrifice. Both are required for true relationship, for love, to grow.

Two, God will never allow us to go over the edge of what we can endure. First Corinthians 10:13 promises that God "will not let you be tempted beyond what you can bear . . . so that you can stand up under it."

So how does this jell with praying not to be led into temptation? Exactly as Peterson renders it—protect us from ourselves, from the selfish, silly, impulsive things we do. And protect us from our Enemy, the one who "prowls around like a roaring lion looking for someone to devour" (1 Peter 5:8).

Formal Versus Free Verse

Out of the riches of Christ's instruction, my question as a fourth-grade student remains: *How* should we pray? Should we pray the Lord's Prayer exactly as Jesus cited it, or is it more of a model of how we are to pray? Are some ways of praying better than others? Is there a place for prewritten, preplanned prayers? Or should all prayer be spontaneous?

Most biblical scholars fall into one of these two camps. One group believes that the Lord's Prayer was given as a specific form prayer, much like Old Testament and rabbinical prayers, and it should be used liturgically. The other group believes that the prayer is really no more than an outline. While it can be prayed repetitively, it is simply an example of how to approach our Father and effectively communicate with Him. This group points to my grandmother's reference, Jesus' admonition: "And when you are praying, do not use meaningless repetition, as the Gentiles do, for they suppose that they will be heard for their many words" (Matthew 6:7, NASB).

This pointed warning seems to go against the first view that holds the Lord's Prayer inherently magical just because Christ spoke it. It also seems unlikely that Jesus would spend his life ministry exemplifying the gospel through His actions and then give us a prayer formula that smacked of the Old Law. The key phrase in Matthew 6:7 seems to be "meaningless repetition." In other words, repetition yields results. However, when our only goal is to inflate the word count, as if God were weighing our prayers like freshman compositions, we're only becoming Pharisees lost in the appearance of good. No, I believe the Lord's Prayer, while it can sustain us for a lifetime if we pray it sincerely and passionately, is intended more as an example than a formula.

My experience with poetry and creative writing underscores this. Most poems either follow a specific pattern or else they simply follow the design — however loose or unstructured that may be — of the poet. An English sonnet, for example, is a fourteen-line poem with a specific rhyme scheme: abab cdcd efef gg. There's a definite rhythm and meter, usually iambic pentameter, to follow. You can write whatever you want to write, but it must fit within this form. I think of writing poetry as similar to pouring water into a vase.

Writing a free-verse poem, on the other hand, is more like nurturing the growth of a tree. Although we may prune or shape it, the tree grows at its own rate, shaped by the wind, water, and other natural forces. In the same way, free-verse poetry may or may not incorporate the elements particular to formal verse—rhyme, meter, alliteration. Most writers and poets seem to agree, though, that the best free verse writers emerge from a knowledge of form. We need to know the form, and then we can explore the freedom of language. The same is true with prayer, hence the poetry lesson.

When I was a new Christian, some mature believers gave me instruction on how to pray, on what they read and thought and did while they prayed. It helped me to memorize the Lord's Prayer and other classic prayers of devotion. However, I soon yearned for language closer to the words I used in conversation and found myself simply talking to my Father. I needed to explore my own sense of prayerful communication in order to grow in my relationship with God.

I do believe we should pursue both formal and spontaneous prayers, but above all, we should seek honest communication with our Father. If that means reciting the Lord's Prayer three times because our hearts are so heavy and our heads so muddled that we don't have the language to articulate our own prayers, then so be it. In fact, the Lord's Prayer or other prayers of devotion often help us pray through those difficult, indescribable times. Using formal prayer becomes a way for me to communicate despite my inability to speak. Formal and liturgical prayers often allow the Holy Spirit to "[help me] in [my] weakness. We do not know what we ought to pray for, but the Spirit himself intercedes for us with groans that words cannot express" (Romans 8:26).

Often silence is best in such moments; other times form prayers richly capture our feelings, thoughts, and desires.

Prayers of Pride

God desires us to be spontaneous, authentic, and unceasing in our communication with Him. If we take a cursory look at when and where Jesus prayed, we find His life saturated with contact with His Father. Of thirty-one recorded accounts of Jesus' personal prayer life, we find Him praying alone (Matthew 14:23, Mark 1:35, Luke 5:16), with His disciples (Matthew 6:9, Luke 9:18, John 17:1), and in public (Matthew

14:19, 15:36, 27:46; John 11:41). We find our Savior praying in all kinds of physical and emotional states—weariness (Mark 1:35), hunger (Matthew 14:19), thankfulness (Luke 6:12), and sadness to the point of desperation (Matthew 26:36-42). Jesus clearly prayed in diverse settings and moods, but two elements pervade them all: His relationship to God the Father and His humility.

It's easy to view Jesus' standard of prayer, like His standard of living, as perfect and therefore unattainable. While that's true on one level, it's also true that His standard of prayer is perhaps the most accessible way for us to be like Him.

It reminds me of a conversation I had recently with a friend who knew I was working on this book. He asked, "Do you ever wonder how spiritual giants like Brother Lawrence prayed? Or even more contemporary writers like C. S. Lewis or Henri Nouwen? I wonder sometimes if their prayer lives were so far above yours and mine."

"Speak for yourself," I said, jokingly, and knew exactly what he meant. I've wondered the same thing. While I certainly believe that the more spiritually mature the believer, the more the person knows and experiences about prayer, I also firmly hold that all of us are called to pray with the same frequency and fervency as our favorite spiritual mentors. Of course this takes discipline, commitment, and practice. But when we're fostering a relationship with God, not carrying out a contractual agreement, our desire to pray grows exponentially.

The spiritual giants all model Christ's humility in the way they address the Holy One. Rather than clenching their fists tighter around their concerns, their hands open ever wider, trusting God more and more. Whether we follow a formal prayer or our own improvisation, the essence of our prayer should be similarly humble. This isn't easy since our selfishness often gets in the way. Jesus reinforces the importance of our heart's attitude in prayer in His parable depicting two men praying in the synagogue.

> "Two men went up into the temple to pray, one a Pharisee, and the other a tax-gatherer. The Pharisee stood and was praying thus to himself, 'God, I thank Thee that I am not like other people: swindlers, unjust, adulterers, or even like this tax-gatherer. I fast twice a week; I pay tithes of all that I get.' "But the tax-gatherer,

standing some distance away, was even unwilling to lift up his
eyes to heaven, but was beating his breast, saying, 'God, be merciful to me, the sinner!' "I tell you, this man went down to his
house justified rather than the other; for everyone who exalts
himself shall be humbled, but he who humbles himself shall be
exalted." (Luke 18:10-14, NASB)

What is your immediate response to this story of sharp contrasts?
It's easy to view the elitism, classism, and arrogance of the Pharisee and
say, "I'm glad I'm not like him!" and put ourselves immediately in his
place. This parable is not just a simple case of "do this and don't do
that." In fact, the Pharisee is a thoroughly religious man; like many
churchgoers today he tithes, prays, serves, leads, and commits. He feels
deeply about what it means to love God, to be a godly man. The tax
collector, on the other hand, was likely stuck in his dead-end position
and would go back to skimming money off the top of his collections
after his Sabbath experience.

And is the Pharisee's prayer really that selfish? Maybe it's just cultural—a lot of Jewish prayers of gratitude begin the same way. Haven't
we all had the experience of seeing a homeless person and thinking,
"There but for the grace of God go I"? Is that so terrible? Shouldn't we
be grateful for the life He gives us? So what makes the Pharisee so bad,
bad enough for Jesus to pronounce his attitude inferior to that of the low-
life tax man?

As writer Paul Duke explains, "There is a word in his [the
Pharisee's] prayer that is outside the Jewish form, and that one little
word gives him away. He doesn't give thanks that God has spared him
from being a thief, rogue, adulterer, or tax collector; he gives thanks that
he is not *like* them. Here he crosses from the grammar of gratitude into
the grammar of elitism. It's the competitive sideward glance that distorts
prayer." [4] This prideful superiority punctures all of the positives the
Pharisee has going for him.

As we see in Jesus' other encounters with the Pharisees, they were
typically more concerned with fulfilling the law than with relating to
the living God; more intent on management through legalism than
their dependence on His mercy and grace.

Prayers of pride allow us to maintain the pretense of prayer, but the words carry only empty echoes, not the weight of our souls.

Incense on the Altar

Recently I cleaned out a bathroom cabinet and found an old bottle of expensive cologne. When my wife gave it to me several years ago, it was my favorite, redolent of cedar and pine. Opening the bottle now, however, I found its flat aroma sour and unpleasant. It reminded me of the way my prayer life becomes when I don't pursue new methods. I begin feeling tired and stale with God. I dread having to keep my appointed time with Him.

What I long for instead, and what I know God desires, is the sweet aroma of my heart in love with Him. My comparison echoes Revelation 5:8, which describes the "prayers of the saints" as "golden bowls full of incense." Our prayers should be devoid of pride and legalism, and filled instead with the honesty of our heart's true desire for connection with the Father. Our love becomes a sweet aroma, pleasing to Him who so loves us.

How do we live this out? How can our prayers be as spontaneous as a spring shower and as humble and thoughtful as the Lord's Prayer? Consider the way we keep our human relationships vital and enjoyable. We seek both a consistency—a stability built on trust—and a love that deepens with the freshness of each encounter. The same is true of how we relate to our Father. Whether we're relying on someone else's words or creating a poetic language of our own, it's the expression of our heart-attitude that matters most. Therefore, we must not allow our prayer lives to become stale, rote, or too predictable. How we vary the ways, times, and places we communicate with God will depend on each individual.

Perhaps you could take the afternoon off and go on a prayer walk through a city park. Or consider reading through a book of contemporary poems in a coffee shop and praying the poet's words with your own groanings of the Spirit. If you are currently only pantomiming your prayers from a devotional, then you should act on the liberating, transcendent freedom to speak creatively to God. Write Him a poem, love letter, or song (one friend calls this her "junk mail" to God). Search for music that conveys what you're feeling toward God and offer it up as communication to Him. Look for artwork or create your own.

If you feel like you're more on the other end of the spectrum, try to find a regular time to meet God. You might seek out a classic book of prayers and read through it to find prayers which best express your heart. Pursue formal prayers not as ends in themselves, but as a means of getting closer to God. This carries over to the physical way we pray. Kneeling, for instance, is something many of us rarely do unless we attend a liturgical church where it is incorporated into the service. However, the physical activity of bowing forces us to consider who we're speaking to and why we're there. Kneeling for its own sake is no better than the Pharisee's prayer of self-righteousness; yet even when we don't feel like it emotionally or physically, kneeling can reveal our heart's true desire for humility, for stillness, and for our Abba's presence and voice.

As we've seen with the Lord's Prayer, it's not so much the words we use as it is how and why we use them. There are times when language is a barrier, when the Spirit within us prays so much more forcefully out of silence. Then there are times when we aren't sure what to pray or where to begin; it feels like riding a bicycle again after a decade of inactivity. That's when relying on another's words can give voice to what we feel but can't articulate. The prayers of others can push the pedals a time or two as we get warmed up again, finding our own rhythm and pace.

I can't instruct you always to kneel when you pray, or always to pray the Lord's Prayer or someone else's. I would advise you to seek variety in your prayer conversations with the Lord, to keep prayer from becoming routine. If you usually pray on the drive into work, make a special effort to seek an hour alone with God this week. If you kneel in prayer for an hour each morning before breakfast, converse with your Father during your lunch break instead.

The prayers at the end of each chapter in this book are included as aids, not as the best prayer for that chapter's topic. Use them or not. The key is the communication; how we communicate definitely affects the message, but should not subvert it.

Write a poem, draw a picture, cook a meal, pray from a collection of other saints' prayers, attend a liturgical church, kneel beside your bed, skip your usual devotional reading and write your own. Consider all the ways you breathe life and passion into your human relationships. Your relationship with your Abba is no less prone to benefit from such care and attention, and is all the more significant for having done so.

Questions for Prayer and Reflection

1. What have you sighed over in your life today? How will you lift those moments to your Father?

2. What is your favorite part of the Lord's Prayer? Make two lists — one of personal, "daily bread" type requests, and the other of larger, more global, "kingdom come" kinds of requests. What do the two have in common? Pray through both lists this week.

3. How would you describe the difference between the Pharisee and the tax-gatherer? Why is it so easy to lapse into the Pharisee's kind of prayer without even realizing how arrogant we've become? What model does the tax-gatherer give us to cultivate in our prayers?

4. Would you say, up to this point in your Christian journey, that you're more of a formal pray-er or a free-verse type? To what do you attribute this (the way you were taught to pray by others, natural tendencies, your personality, understanding of Scripture on prayer)? How do both types facilitate communication with God? Consider new ways to converse with God and keep your relationship fresh and vital.

Father, what can I say in this hour but to cry out
as these disciples cried out, Lord, teach me how to pray. Teach
me my need. Tear away this veil from my eyes
that makes me think I have any adequacy in myself. . . . Give
me rather, this conscious sense of dependence,
this awareness that nothing I do will be of any value
apart from a dependence upon you.
In Jesus' name, Amen.[5]

— RAY C. STEDMAN

OTHER SPOKES ON THE WHEEL

Our silence awkward as broken glass
at our feet, then one voice undoes the quiet
like a cricket at midnight, kindles
a torch of hope with words, passed
to another, and the next, and again,
our odd choir growing like a flame
until even my voice burns comfortably
for these strangers I've known a lifetime.

—"CIRCLE OF PRAYER"

While our communication with God is top priority, prayer is also about how we relate to each other. Prayer unites us in the closest bonds amidst the most joyful or horrendous or mundane circumstances. A recent experience comes to mind.

Prayers of the Disrupters

The first class I taught at a Christian university did not go well. Since I was also teaching at a large state university, I expected my Christian class to be completely liberating, full of eager young men and women who not only desired to learn something about writing, but were hungry for more of Christ in their lives as well.

The first big difference I noticed was that the Christian students were fresh-from-high-school eighteen-year-olds, many away from home for the first time. This contrasted sharply with my state university nontraditional student body composed of many full-time workers, parents, and other folks juggling numerous responsibilities. These students stimulated enjoyable classes because of their maturity, focus, and diversity.

My class of Christians, on the other hand, contained diversity, but it felt more divisive. Some of the students were very shy but attempted to "spiritualize" everything in their essay topics and class discussions. They soon formed a clique and seemed to hold the rest of the class in contempt. Several student athletes formed another clique and made it clear they didn't care much about our class or about appearing spiritual. A couple of believers stood out for beliefs that seemed remarkably liberal compared to their peers.

Another clique formed as the worst amalgam of all the groups; I labeled them the "Disrupters." They constantly spoke out, tried to sleep, or diverted attention away from our discussion toward last night's basketball game, the latest music video, or what their church was planning that weekend. They ignored my authority as best they could.

Don't get me wrong, I run a laid-back classroom. I base my authority on respect and I expect to earn it. Nevertheless, I found myself dreading the noon hour when my class would convene, hating the inevitable disciplinary conflicts and the lack of focus on writing. In fact, several students after class one day pleaded with me to take stronger measures with the Disrupters so that those who wanted to learn could learn.

Then I accidentally discovered that many professors prayed at the beginning of their classes or read a short devotional. Many students found this rote and predictable. I decided to give it a try since dynamics seemed to be going from bad to worse.

I wondered if the students would dismiss me or humor me or view praying in class as nothing more than a technique to shame them into cooperation. On a Monday afternoon, I took roll and then tentatively read a passage from one of my favorite writers, Frederick Buechner. I then immediately asked for prayer requests, for areas of concern.

"I'll be honest," I said. "I'm really struggling with how best to teach and lead this class. I ask for your prayers to help me bring us together as a focused classroom community, not an unruly group forced to endure something we all hate." Raised eyebrows. Curious glances. A weighty silence.

One young woman lifted her hand and asked for prayer for her mother, dying of cancer. Another student raised his hand and confessed that he was really struggling with his dorm roommate. Another woman wanted to thank God for providing a last-minute scholarship for her. Miraculously, over half the class sought prayer concerning requests weighing on their minds and hearts—everything from finances to jobs, friends to dying parents.

And they prayed for each other, too. I gave them the freedom to pray silently or aloud and volunteered to close after a few minutes. We prayed for at least fifteen minutes! We spent well over half our class time taking requests and praying, but it was more than worth it. Not just because it restored a new kind of order. More importantly, it brought us together as people, not just as the roles we were forced to play as professor and students, but as men and women, hoping and longing, scared and afraid to open up, to share our struggles, requests, and praises.

We continued the habit for the rest of the semester, and I was fascinated to see the change in classroom dynamics. Unsolicited, students would ask each other about their requests, about their lives and what they were experiencing of our Father. My Disrupters became better students and grew in compassion and love for one another. Through the power of the Holy Spirit, we cut through the pretense of prayer and found a place to come together and corporately experience the body of Christ asking, seeking, loving God and each other.

Necessary Risks

Relationships are essential for human development and spiritual growth. Our Father designed us this way. Consequently, our prayers reflect a relational dimension as well. Perhaps this seems obvious, at least cognitively and theologically. The painful reality remains that many of us would rather not risk our fears, secrets, and hopes with one another.

Why would God command us to seek out and cultivate something we long for at the deepest part of our being? Shouldn't it be natural to do so? It is natural, of course. We want to know and love other people and be known and loved by them; after our desire for God, it is our greatest longing. The primary command of Christ after "love the Lord your God with all your heart and with all your soul and with all your mind" (Matthew 22:37), is to love others: "A new command I give you: Love one another. As I have loved you, so you must love one another" (John 13:34).

However, carrying out this command proves exceedingly difficult for most of us. When we try to manipulate people to get what we want, it usually backfires at some point. When we love selflessly and sacrificially, we can still end up getting hurt.

I think of a friend's struggle with some of his closest friends: "I started asking myself why I do it—why I risk and risk and hope and trust and pray for relationships here on earth. My wife recently asked the same question. She and I went so far as to do a little Bible study on this issue of friendships."

I asked, "So what did you come up with?"

"The best reason to pursue people in relationships is because Jesus did. Because God pursues us. That's about it."

We both laughed at the painful awareness this conclusion cut in us as well as the hope that followed. It hurts to be in relationship with others, yet God consistently, supernaturally, uses all of us, despite ourselves, to be Christ to each other.

Prayer can be a lifelong bridge in providing connections with others. In fact, Scripture makes it clear that we grow in love by praying *with* one another as well as *for* one another. Jesus prays with the disciples repeatedly (Matthew 6:9, 11:25; Luke 9:18, 22:39-40; John 17:1). We're reminded to pray together (Acts 1:14; Matthew 18:20). We're exhorted to pray for one another (Colossians 1:9; James 5:16).

Shared Voices

Unfortunately, praying together often divides believers rather than brings them closer together. It may be subtle, but most of us at some time have felt the awkward tension of being forced to pray aloud with others. Instead of concentrating on the shared relationship we have with our Father, instead of addressing Him, we turn inward. Group prayer becomes a competition, a contest to determine who is most eloquent and who is most spiritual. This competitive spirit often makes it difficult to overcome self-conscious prayer with other people. It becomes a speech class where we're all grading each other's diction, eloquence, and articulation. We judge others and try to one-up their best prayer. The proper focus on God is lost and shifted back to us once more.

At a recent conference, during such a corporate prayer time, one man prayed a very eloquent and sophisticated prayer. At one point he said, "Lord, help us to overcome—no, not to overcome but to work through—our obstacles at this conference." His aside felt canned, like reading a cue card. Being the cynical, competitive Pharisee that I am, I opened my eyes to check if he was reading his prayer. At that point I became very sad for myself.

How do we overcome such self-centeredness? How do we share our deepest concerns with others? First, we assess the context of our relationship with those with whom we're praying. Second, we focus on our relationship with God, not on evaluating everyone else's. Sharing our prayers is one of the most vulnerable activities we do on this earth. I believe it's more private than eating or making love.

When Mother Teresa was once asked to comment on her personal relationship with Christ, she blushed and said that she couldn't find the words to describe such a personal relationship. If you ask me to describe my wife, and our relationship, I might try—"Dotti is tender and beautiful and funny and smart and knows God in ways I don't and mothers our children so graciously, and she has such a stunning quality about her that is all her own, her Dottiness, as I jokingly refer to it"—but I can truly never come close to putting words to this woman and what she means to me, and how I love her.

Similarly, we cannot fully describe our relationship with our Abba Father. Too often, I believe, we lose much of the mystery, passion, and intimacy we experience and long for by being too quick to put words to it, too quick to share it inappropriately. We make it too familiar, too commonplace, a cliché of faith rather than an ineffable poem of our hearts and spirits. Imagine me walking up to a busy intersection in New York and telling a stranger, "Let me tell you how much I love my wife— she is so incredible!" No context exists for either my sharing or my audience's reception of such an ineffable kind of love. In our information-glutted age I believe we have to spend more time loving and communicating with God privately before we begin sharing about it with others. We must cultivate intimacy with God individually before we attempt it corporately in prayer with others.

As we explore our passion for our Father, our relational passion for others grows exponentially. Recall the way Jesus loved the unlovely and always made time for lepers, outcasts, and children. The love He experienced with the Father empowered and inspired Him to love all peoples: "When he saw the crowds, he had compassion on them, because they were harassed and helpless, like sheep without a shepherd" (Matthew 9:36). To pray with another person opens us up to them and them to us. We find ourselves bridged by a relationship we both have in common yet experience uniquely and individually. Our shared voices create a symphony of prayer before our loving Conductor.

Other Spokes

The second aspect of relational prayer, praying for others, is often like breathing. If you love someone, you know what it is for their face or voice to surface across your memory and for your only loving response to be to lift them up before the One who loves them more than you. If we love people, then we don't have to be told what it's like to feel powerless, helpless, angry, sad, or thrilled because of that bond to another human life

Praying for other people is perhaps the most powerful, loving, influential relational activity we can perform for someone. It takes our eyes off of ourselves and onto the needs and concerns of others. We step back from our spotlight of self-centeredness and illuminate the needs of others. Praying for others reminds us of our connection to the vast fabric of humanity. Despite how lonely and isolated we often feel, we are not alone. Not only do we have God, we have each other.

Consider the way a wheel is designed. There's the hub, which is often what we consider ourselves, the center of our own little universe. The spokes represent all the different relationships we have with others; each one is unique and specific, but they combine to form a relational network. Finally, there's the perimeter of the wheel that holds everything together, connecting the hub and spokes with something bigger. This represents God's design for our lives and relationships, a pattern we cannot always see from our hub-perspective. This illustration reminds us of our need to trust and believe in our Father's ultimate willful design for our lives. The comparison also reminds us of our connections to other spokes on the wheel. We are inextricably linked to other people. The circumstances vary, but the depth of the human condition with all its joys, sorrows, fears, and hopes remains consistent across cultures and throughout time.

Intercessory prayer allows us to tap into this depth — to care for one another as individuals, as family members. One of the things I love about the liturgical aspect of the Episcopal Church is the time of intercession incorporated into every service. These prayers usually begin by praying for large groups of people — world leaders, presidents, church leaders — and working their way down to local concerns. Finally, worshipers are given the chance to voice their own prayers simply by speaking a person's first name. "At this time let us lift up the names of those on our hearts and minds," says the priest. Throughout the congregation solo voices whisper a name or speak it loudly, usually only a first name. And we lift each other's loved ones and enemies up together, even though we know nothing more than a first name and maybe the bowed head that spoke it.

I think of an early morning service I attended in the beautiful little chapel at Saint John's in Knoxville, Tennessee. This particular morning service was sparsely attended, and during the intercession time I was struck by one white-haired woman's concern as she listed names, " . . . James . . . Shannon . . . Carrie . . . Tom . . . Susan . . . Bill . . . Sarah . . . Julie . . ." She probably went on to list at least another dozen names. There was a physical dimension to her furrowed brow and tightly shut eyes, a quiet strength in her voice, a lifetime of faith mapped across her wrinkled face, as she knelt on a hard, cold kneeler on a rainy Monday morning. Something in me longed to have this saint pray for me and for me to pray for my short list with the same fervor and passionate hope with which she prayed.

Holy Privilege
Richard Foster says that "we are responsible before God to pray for those God brings into our circle of nearness. With Samuel of old we say, 'God forbid that I should sin against the Lord in ceasing to pray for you' (1 Samuel 12:23, KJV)."[1] While this responsibility is shared by all children of the King's kingdom, the way we go about it differs as much as the unique personality doing the praying.

Some friends of mine collect photos of their loved ones, missionary

friends, and even world leaders, and create a bulletin board prayer col-
lage. Other friends make lists and rotate them throughout the week.
Some people pray by simply quieting themselves before the Lord and then
allowing the Holy Spirit to bring people to mind. This is often how I pray
and I'm surprised by the long-lost friend or known-by-name-only person who drifts into my prayer focus.

Recently a former student of mine visited me in the office. We
caught up on each other's lives for the year or two we'd lost. As he was
about to leave he turned and said, "Professor Delffs, this seems kind of
odd. But for the last year I've thought of you so often when I pray. Your
name and face come to mind and I don't have any idea what your need
is, but I pray for you. If you have something specific that I can pray for
you — that's why I'm even bringing this up — I'll be happy to."

"I can think of lots of things," I replied, stunned by grace, by the
unseen forces of God's love. "But for now, just keep praying the way you
have been." I smiled and he smiled and it was a rich moment of connection to each other and to the Father we share.

Fruits of Other-Centered Prayer

We reinforce our desire to know God in two ways when we pray with
others and for others. First, prayer for others cultivates a spirit of *compassion*—a point of transcendent risk that loves others more than self
because of the love of Jesus that He breathes through us. Second, other-
centered prayer produces in us *vision*—a larger sense of God's plan for our
lives and the lives of others. We end up seeing who they are and where
they've come from, but greater still, who they are called to be. We see their
potential — who God wants them to be and wants to shape them to be.

Like faith in Christ and a prayer-centered life, compassion requires
a lifetime to develop. God uses prayer to impart His compassion on us.
He listens, forgives, embraces, chastises, and speaks to our hearts out
of His compassionate love for us. Praying with and for others allows us
to pass on this compassion to others, to demonstrate the Father's love.
Few express this truth more eloquently than Henri Nouwen:

When you pray, you discover not only yourself and God, but
also your neighbor. For in prayer, you profess not only that

people are people and God is God, but also, that your neighbor is your sister or brother living alongside you. For the same conversion that brings you to the painful acknowledgment of your wounded human nature also brings you to the joyful recognition that you are not alone, but that being human means being together.

At precisely this point, compassion is born. Compassion grows with the inner recognition that your neighbor shares your humanity with you. This partnership cuts through all walls which might have kept you separate. Across all barriers of land and language, wealth and poverty, knowledge and ignorance, we are one, created from the same dust, subject to the same laws and destined for the same end.[2]

Such compassion is what we find time and again in Jesus' example and instruction. He shows us what it's like to break the cultural taboos and talk with someone on a lower rung of the societal ladder. Or what it's like to show compassion to a woman caught in adultery and about to be stoned by men just as guilty, in their hearts if not their behavior, as she is. Jesus shows us time and again what it's like to seek out tax collectors, embrace prostitutes, heal lepers, or love the unlovable and unattractive.

His model encourages me to go outside the confines of my comfort and self-consciousness and quit labeling people. For me this means befriending and loving gay people no less than I'm called to relate to my pastor. We certainly make discernments about behavior and consequences, but not about whom to love. God loves all people, giving us chance after chance to respond to His love. For me this means doing something—teaching, feeding, praying, helping—for people who are homeless, or people who have AIDS or cancer. For me this means not judging the wealthy and dismissing them. Jesus' example calls me to transcend the finiteness of my selfish, insecure perceptions and biases and embrace the total human condition. This means praying with and for these people.

Jesus' instruction reinforces this obedience as a manifestation of the love we have for Him and a reflection of the grace we have experienced despite our own unworthiness. Consider the parable of the good Samaritan:

> "There was once a man traveling from Jerusalem to Jericho. On the way he was attacked by robbers. They took his clothes, beat him up, and went off leaving him half-dead. Luckily, a priest was on his way down the same road, but when he saw him he angled across to the other side. Then a Levite religious man showed up; he also avoided the injured man.
>
> A Samaritan traveling the road came on him. When he saw the man's condition, his heart went out to him. He gave him first aid, disinfecting and bandaging his wounds. Then he lifted him on to his donkey, led him to an inn, and made him comfortable. In the morning he took out two silver coins and gave them to the innkeeper, saying, 'Take good care of him. If it costs any more, put it on my bill—I'll pay you on my way back.'" (Luke 10:30-35, MSG)

Jesus told this story in response to being asked by a religious scholar, "Since we are to 'love our neighbors as ourselves,' who is my neighbor?" As you can see, Jesus' response shows our neighbor to be anyone and everyone, especially those we might not naturally be inclined to serve, love, or pray for.

Praying for Enemies

Consider Jesus' exhortation to "love your enemies, do good to those who hate you, bless those who curse you, pray for those who mistreat you" (Luke 6:27-28). He goes on to say how easy it is to love only those who love us, those who please us and conform to our wishes. Everybody does that. Yet to pray for people who wish us ill, who hate us, revile us, misunderstand us, and don't care about us requires suffering and trust in ultimate hope. Once again, without a fundamental grounding in the hope of the Cross, we have nothing supernatural, let alone logical, to motivate or fuel a prayerful love for those with whom we are most uncomfortable.

We see the epitome of this in Christ praying for His enemies as He's nailed onto a wooden cross: "Father, forgive them, for they do not know what they are doing" (Luke 23:34).

Today it often feels like our enemies outnumber our friends. The Enemy uses political divisions, racism, sexism, class differences, cultural barriers, selfishness, and greed to pit us against one another. In a lifetime we all experience prejudice and likely participate in perpetuating it against others. Prayer is an incredible weapon to sever enemy lines. It allows us to "heap burning coals" of kindness on those who persecute us (Proverbs 25:21-22, Romans 12:20-21). It crosses lines of culture, race, gender, and lifestyle to demonstrate the Father's irrational, unfathomable love.

During the course of writing this book, a terrible and unsettling epidemic of arson-related fires claimed almost fifty black churches. Most church leaders as well as arson investigators thought the fires were racially based. But in the midst of this tragic season, more and more racial lines have been crossed and whites and blacks and other races are coming together to pray for an end to the crimes and to begin rebuilding the physical manifestation of what can never be consumed by fire—the Spirit of the church. Ralph Reed, executive director of the mostly white, conservative Christian Coalition said, "We come today bearing the burden of that history [segregation and the battle for civil rights] with broken hearts, a repentant spirit and ready hands to fight this senseless violence."[3]

Prejudice need not be racial to separate peoples. Many of us succumb to spiritual biases in the way we relate to people. We compete with other denominations over doctrine, over numbers ("So, how big is your church?"), or over methodology. I'm not saying there aren't real differences and real discernments to be made. I am saying that we need to see how much more we have in common in the way we love and serve God rather than working hard to conform everyone else to our way of viewing what it means to love and serve God.

When we pray together, God can bind up old wounds and fault lines, rebuild churches and feed hungry children. Praying for people is a rich battle zone of opportunity for us to love in the most powerful way we can. I believe such a prayer-fueled faith comes out of living this way not just in moments of disease or crisis, but all the time, every day. We are to relate to God and others by communicating in word and deed what it is we long for most.

So what does it mean to cultivate other-centered prayer that produces compassion? I believe it means we suffer petty differences, digest our pride, and unite with other people in the commonality of our human condition. When we pray with and for people we're not comfortable with, whether they are enemies, perceived enemies, or simply people who are different than we are, we live out the language of prayer, the alphabet of hope.

One caveat: There are certainly times when we should not share too much too soon. We must respect certain boundaries of context and depth of relationship. However, we must also be willing to take risks — to be vulnerable, to show our true selves and lift each other up.

One of my favorite reminders of this occurred when my wife and I were just beginning to date. I was going through a difficult, reflective, and repentant season of my life and I experienced many dark, moody days. Some of these I'd share with Dotti, but often I withdrew from her under the pretense of "protecting" her from my emotional baggage. I didn't want to risk at such a deep level the issues I was facing and the pain I was feeling, so I would pull away, genuinely yearning to share my heart with her without pressuring her to make me feel better.

One day, after I had not communicated with her for a few days, I found a note with these words taped to my door: "Please do not be afraid to share the tough days as well as the good ones. Or else how will I be able to tell you about mine? How will we know to lift each other to our Father?" Her words stung me by being so simple and direct and incredibly unselfish and loving.

Such communication through prayer allows us to grow in compassion, to risk more of our hearts instead of playing it safe or trying to use people to meet our deepest longing for God. Such compassion swells and replaces our fears and insecurities, our pretensions and posturing, our pride and prejudice. Through the voice of prayer and the eyes of compassion, we see and love people as God sees and loves us.

X-Ray Visions

Another way to see others as God does is to cultivate a view that sees people as works in progress. As Paul wrote in Ephesians 2:10, "We are God's workmanship, created . . . to do good works." The workmanship word here is *poiema,* or "poem." Our Father views us both as who we are in the present (and where we've come from) and also as who we are becoming. What does it mean for us to cultivate a vision of who someone is and of his or her true potential? First, we must have compassion for that person and then we must do our best to know the person as they are and as God calls them to be.

As I recall my short-lived counseling career, I remember observing time and again the tension of what people really wanted from therapy: the freedom to show their worst self, their most unloving selfish darkness, and for the counselor (or anyone) not to turn and run from it. (And the freedom to show their best, warmest, most Spirit-filled self and have that affirmed.)

We want to be known and loved for who we are, not rejected for our mistakes, deficits, or shortcomings. The only way to extend this to each other, of course, is to experience it first in the arms of Jesus. To find Him running breathlessly toward us as we prostitute ourselves to idols, even as we spit at Him and whimper, "Please, leave me alone. I'm no good. Not even You can help. Please." And He cuts through the selfishness and our attempts to keep Him at arm's length. He holds us tight and never lets us go. Then we're free to do the same as we relate with others.

When we have a vision for people we can pray more deeply and more transcendently than simply praying for their immediate circumstances. We can pray for character issues, for marriages and families, for their relationships with God. This kind of vision is often the essence of sustaining a loving relationship.

Think about the people Jesus chose for His disciples. As many writers and scholars have pointed out, they were not the wealthy, the most educated, successful, powerful, even attractive men of their day. They were common and fallible, fishermen for the most part, who had the most important thing going for them—faith, hope, and love for and in this strange leader who touched their hearts. Jesus saw who they could be, not who they were. He saw beyond the denial of Peter, the doubts of Thomas, even beyond the betrayal of Judas, and devoted Himself to these men with a love that saw beyond their present condition. They became men of faith—leaders, hopers, dreamers who participated in the foundation of God's most magnificent plan of redemption, initiating the history of Christ's body, the church.

Even in the Old Testament, time and again we see God persevering with people because He sees them as more than just the sum of their failures and shortcomings. He turns reluctant speakers like Moses into leaders of nations. He turns childless couples like Abraham and Sarah into the forebears of countless generations. He redeems tricksters like Jacob into a new being, into a man with a new name, the father of an entire nation. God sees behind the Saul in all of us and calls with Jesus' voice to become the Paul we are meant to be.

How does this vision transfer to praying for others? The picture of visionary prayer in practice is often blurry. In addition to compassion it requires imagination channeled in love. The vision I have for my wife helps me pray for her immediate need—that her friendships with other women continue to bloom—but also for her development in the likeness of Christ—that she'll know God better and deeper and richer because of the way she and these friends love each other.

As I pray for my wife, I often imagine her as a beautiful old woman one day inviting young mothers to lunch and telling them stories about how she raised her children, how she came to love her husband through difficult times, or what it was like when she lost her own mother to cancer. This vision is not only scriptural (see Titus 2:3-5), but it stems from who my wife is, the kinds of things she likes, the people she is drawn to. Such a vision carves in me a deep longing for my wife, for her fulfillment not just of her own desires, but beyond the limits of her own and my own imagination to the place where God touches her and embraces her as His perfected daughter.

All of us need people in our lives who love us enough not to let us stay the way we are. Yes, they first accept and love us where we are in the present, just as our Father does. But they don't settle for less than who we are meant to be. They see the creative flair in the way we write a letter or decorate a room. They see the strength needed to lead a Bible study or compromise with others. They have a kind of X-ray vision that cuts through our petty, selfish desires for comfort, convenience, and the easy life our culture and media dangles before us. Vision-praying friends pray for God's will in our lives, His work in our lives, even at the expense of what we ourselves think we want. They see beyond what we'd like, what they'd like, to a God who loves better, despite appearances from our lopsided view.

Other-centered prayer allows us to fully reflect the tension of being human as well as being redeemed. We have a loving compassion for others that transcends competition, jealousy, or the painful relational disappointments that all of us suffer at times. By cultivating a prayerful vision of who people can be and are called to be, we fight isolation and promote unity and love with the love of Christ. When we've tasted the limitless meal our Father spreads before us, it becomes easy to share from the table with others. We are moved to give out of what we've been given.

Praying for others is perhaps one of the most intimate acts of love we can do for one another. It keeps us centered in communication with our Father who loves each of us equally, without end.

Questions for Prayer and Reflection

1. Which is more difficult for you to do, pray with someone or pray for someone? What are you risking in each instance?

2. What is your greatest barrier in cultivating compassion for other people? List people groups that you know you struggle to love. Try to pray from your present position for God to draw you closer to loving these people through Him, through the Holy Spirit.

3. Pray that God would allow you to know the sufferings of your brothers and sisters, especially those listed above, as your own.

4. Can you think of someone who has had a vision for you that made a difference in the way you lived and saw yourself? Describe this person's impact on your life. Think of three people and journal about who they could be if they sought God at any cost. Ask your Father to reveal to you a glimpse of each person's unique potential and pray that it will grow and yield fruit.

5. Find at least one other friend to pray with this week. Share what you've been thinking and feeling as you read this chapter. Commit to praying together at least one more time soon.

*Lord, teach me to respect people, to accept each person
as unique and created by you. Some people seem so
unattractive that I find it extremely difficult to see you
in them. Yet if I could see myself as others see me,
perhaps I would be less critical and more understanding. Of
your goodness give me compassion for myself
and for others, and never let me give up trying
for the sake of your Son, who genuinely loved
and cared about sinners and outcasts.*[4]

— MICHAEL HOLLINGS AND ETTA GULLICK

PART THREE

DIVINE DIALOGUE: PRAYERS OF PURPOSE

If by prayer
Incessant I could hope to change the will
Of him who all things can, I would not cease
To weary him with my assiduous cries.
　　—MILTON, PARADISE LOST

If you abide in Me,
and My words abide in you,
ask whatever you wish,
and it shall be done for you.
　　—JOHN 15:7 (NASB)

Praise the LORD, all nations:
Laud Him, all peoples!
For His lovingkindness is great toward us,
And the truth of the LORD is everlasting,
Praise the LORD!
　　—PSALM 117 (NASB)

TRUE CONFESSIONS

Sometimes, confessing, I incise
the skin over my breast-bone, between
my breasts, press the bone-saw's
intolerable teeth through
the knotting of sternum and ribs,
excavate the narrow valley floor
even deeper, open the vein of gold
that branches up from my mother lode,
unearth my molten heart for you, and
your dark, delicate, intrusive mining.[1]

— LUCI SHAW

Imagine a dark, claustrophobic small room. A tall man with beard stubble and a side arm blows cigarette smoke in your face and says, "We know what you did. You might as well make it easy on yourself and tell the truth. Let's have your confession." You're forced into breaking down and spilling out the long story that brought you to this place.

It's a typical ending to many mystery stories, yet reflects what sometimes happens in real life in our relationship with God. We break the law because we're selfish. We get caught or we're overcome with guilt. We tell the truth about what happened, *ending* with confession of our sin instead of beginning with it.

Finding a Formula

As a new Christian I used a devotional guide that encouraged me to structure my prayer with a time-honored pattern: A(doration), C(onfession), T(hanksgiving), S(upplication)—ACTS for short. This is a highly respected, biblical outline of communication. I followed it for several months but began to notice my interest waning. As I examined my prayer process, I discovered two problems with my use of ACTS.

First, it quickly became rote. Yet I felt obligated to use the ACTS devotional formula because it was popular with my other Christian friends. While it was good to have a regular pattern to follow, I quickly put my emphasis on completing each phase of the process rather than on communicating with my Father. This shift was certainly my problem, not the pattern's. Unfortunately, we all struggle with this problem. As humans we want a formula, a way to know how to pray, when to pray, what to pray — usually for selfish motives to attain what we want for ourselves and others or to feel a certain way. Thus, we turn prayer into incantation, a magic formula that should produce our desires every time.

One friend describes this struggle: "It's such an easy shift from God's will to my will. I believe we all want to get what we pray for. We also want to experience those transcendent moments of intimacy with God, those warm feelings, every time we pray. It's like trying to force each conversation we have with a human friend into a Vulcan mind-meld — to be a perfect connection. But that feeling becomes the emphasis, not the exchange of communication."

As we saw in Chapter Five, prayer forms and techniques often provide structure, discipline, and guidelines for communicating with God. They can facilitate a consistency in our prayers, a regular engagement of our hearts so that our lives become increasingly centered in prayerful dialogue with our Abba Father.

Methods such as ACTS are often wonderful ways to begin to structure our prayer lives. However, we must guard against becoming more focused on technique than on the conversation itself. To keep my prayer life fresh and alive, I needed to loosen up and become more natural in my approach to God rather than feel like I always had to follow a formal protocol.

Saved from Death Row

The second lesson I learned from this experience was that confession often needs to be the first step in prayer. It was difficult for me to begin with adoration when I was preoccupied with my sins. I felt like a guilty child trying to enjoy dinner while knowing that I deserved a spanking.

My self-centered focus would not allow me to fully adore my Creator for who He is. I first needed to tell Him what He already knew and embrace the love He always extends.

On good days, I so desire a rightness with God that I must begin by confessing my faults and asking forgiveness. Confession then releases movement into other modes of prayer.

Confession remains a humbling place of prayerful renewal. Recently, I was struck by a character's comment in a short story: "Advice is what we ask for when we already know the answer, but wish we didn't." The same is true of confession. We often avoid, ignore, or deny confession because it forces us to a broken-hearted stance before our Father.

Isn't this loving forgiveness what we all long for? To be forgiven and pardoned from the death-row sentence of our sin and shame? Of course, and of course not. In that deep, tender spot in our hearts, we so long for it that the place always feels like a sponge thirsty for more living water. At the same time, our pride and self-absorption affects our willingness to be helpless before the most awesome Power in the universe. In confession we are at our most vulnerable. We are naked in the garden, longing for restoration but hiding behind shabby hedges of our own making. We are at the foot of the cross, lifting up sour wine-vinegar to the innocent Christ and simultaneously whispering, "Jesus, remember me when You come in into Your kingdom!"

Confession forces us to relinquish the self-justifying dialogue with ourselves and address what is true. We are murderers, prostitutes, thieves, cheaters, liars, bigots, idolaters. We confess: I hated my friend this week because he didn't call me . . . I lied about my motives for wanting to spend time with You . . . I worshiped an idol last night because I wanted the immediate gratification that buying a new suit provided . . . I withdrew my heart from my wife when she questioned my decision about money . . . I remained silent at work to be accepted when I should have spoken up.

I worshiped so many false gods—approval of others, success, money, pleasure—that I could move about like chess pieces rather than face the living God.

Confession fuels repentance and opens the dialogue between us and our Abba Father and addresses what is true. Through confession we realize that we are loved more for who we are than what we do, that we are forgiven, that God gives Himself to us every day. Our Father loves and forgives us every day in a mystery of passion that never grows tired or predictable. He knows what we've done, how we've failed, but is eager to embrace us and restore our relationship.

Frederick Buechner writes, "To confess your sins to God is not to tell him anything he doesn't already know. Until you confess them, however, they are the abyss between you. When you confess them, they become the bridge."[2]

Confession continually reduces our inflated sense of self that comes from the remnants of our sinful nature. Confession regrounds us in the liberating freedom of humility, giving us a child's remembrance of needing the Father. Admitting our faults and asking for grace reestablishes our relationship with God and reminds us of a loving passion superior to any we can imagine. Confession epitomizes forgiveness in the face of the unforgivable.

We experience such grace from the Father of the prodigal, running to greet all of us selfish, debauched children limping with shame, and perhaps, somewhere a glimmer of hope that the confrontation won't go as badly as we deserve. After confession our glimmer of hope turns into a blazing supernova beyond our wildest dreams. We are bathed in a transforming Love, the love of a Father who gave up His tenderest passion for His most troublesome passion.

The love of Christ mirrors this same passion. Jesus experienced the sweat and stench of human existence, facing every emotion you or I hoard in self-pity. Drawing on faith in His Father's love, Jesus willingly entered a death that separated Him from that very love in order to take our place on death row. Such a passionate sacrifice fuels the flame in the Lover's eyes for His beloved.

No matter how we try to describe this love, our words are inadequate. It is the experience that counts—the risk of confessing daily, the act of living out of grace. In his exquisite, contemporary novel, *Atticus*, Ron Hansen updates the parable of the prodigal son. Scott Cody is a rebel artist, a restless spirit who has drank, slept, and spent his way through the first half of his life. As a college student, he drove recklessly in a Colorado snowstorm; the car crashed into a telephone pole and claimed the life of his only passenger, his mother. Scott's father, Atticus, is miraculously able to forgive his son this gravest of trespasses. The communication between them, though, suffers the painful distance between father and son, with neither able to articulate his need or his gift of love. With Scott home for a Christmas visit, the father reflects on what he desperately wants to speak to his son's heart:

> Were Atticus to talk honestly, he thought, he'd say he was alone all the time and this was his son whom he loved and ached for, and heaven was where *he* was, and Atticus hated himself, as he always did, for insisting and teaching and holding up standards and seeming to want Scott to be him, when all he wanted was for Scott to be happy and to know he was loved and loved and loved.[3]

Cornerstone of Communication

Our heavenly Father extends the same loving forgiveness to us. In addition to the restoration of our relationship with Him, confession opens us up to the other modes of prayer. As a prayerful acknowledgment of our helplessness, confession actualizes true humility and reminds us of our soul-hunger for the Bread of Life instead of the crummy pig-slop we typically feed ourselves.

It's not easy to begin prayer with confession. In fact, it may be one of the most difficult aspects of prayer because of the humility it requires. Its significance to prayer cannot be underestimated. Confession is the cornerstone of communication with God. It is where we reestablish the connection we so desperately long for. After confession there's a restored confidence and freedom to bring our petitions before Him; there's a renewed passion to praise and adore Him.

One caution: We should not view confession as a prerequisite self-abasement so that we can feel good about the rest of our prayer time. If we take such a self-centered approach, we end up emphasizing once again the technique rather than the content of our prayers. True confession is a conversation about the state of our relationship with God. True confession is an acknowledgment that we can't really talk about other things on our mind until we've removed the obvious barriers.

The fact is, we need to confess our sins and renew our sense of God's grace every day. The cry of confession is not something to be postponed until the account is past due. It's a continual daily exercise. While we have the security of salvation through the presence of Christ in our lives, our sinful nature continues to dog us as it reluctantly yields to the transforming power of the Holy Spirit.

Our resistance to the helplessness and humility of confession is one of the greatest barriers to maintaining a rich prayer garden. Whether we've murdered someone or simply stabbed their reputation, whether we've wallowed in adultery or merely fantasized, all of us are in the sinners' boat together. The only life preserver from this sinking ship is God's grace. Nevertheless, we have to embrace this gift, not merely take it for granted (see Romans 6) or run from it, too proud and self-sufficient to accept what we need and long for most. Our response to grace must be an open-armed embrace that renews our hearts and changes our lives.

Annie Dillard writes, "It is so self-conscious, so apparently moral, simply to step aside from the gaps where the creeks and winds pour down, saying, I never merited this grace, quite rightly, and then to sulk along the rest of your days on the edge of rage. I won't have it." She concludes, "The world is wilder than that in all directions, more dangerous and bitter, more extravagant and bright."[4]

I would add that our Father's love is deeper and wilder than we typically imagine. Like a buoy thrown to a drowning person, grace must be embraced, recognized for what it is—a gift that compels us into life with gratitude and love.

Changing Course

There's a cause-effect relationship between confession and repentance. *Confess* means "to admit, to tell." *Repent* means "to turn, to change course." As a result of the sorrow over our sinfulness and the subsequent joy over God's embrace from the midst of our condition (and this is not necessarily a quick movement), we live out a life of loving devotion. Like King David excavating his sin with Bathsheba and all that followed, we cut through our self-defenses and admit, "Against Thee, Thee only, I have sinned, and done what is evil in Thy sight" (Psalm 51:4, NASB).

We acknowledge our helplessness and release the deepest desire of our heart: "Create in me a clean heart, O God, and renew a steadfast spirit within me. . . . Restore to me the joy of Thy salvation, and sustain me with a willing spirit" (Psalm 51:10,12, NASB). Or, it is like the woman who washes Jesus' feet with her tears and anoints them with costly perfume (Luke 7:36-50).

Our only response to grace is to change our actions. We no longer live to fulfill our selfish impulses but to love our Father and those around us. Such changes in behavior are not easy. I do not want to make light of the struggle between the flesh, our old sinful nature, and our spirit, which is being renewed in Christ's likeness. This tension is the arena where most of us live out our faith, day by day. Like Paul in his letter to the Romans (chapter 7), we ask, "Why do I do what I don't want to do?" We must wrestle over and over with temptations and failures, with confession and grace, until the angel blesses us like Jacob and we limp away until the next day's battle. However, it is so easy to get distracted by the struggle that we often lose sight of what we already have access to. Paul offers us hope in the same chapter of Romans: "Who will rescue me from this body of death? Thanks be to God— through Jesus Christ our Lord! . . . . Therefore, there is now no condemnation for those who are in Christ Jesus" (7:24-25,8:1).

What keeps us focused on the struggle rather than on our relationship with the Father? Once again, pride rears its ugly head. The Enemy knows how to use us against ourselves. Pride keeps us from accepting the grace so freely extended to us by a loving Father. Pride is the tenacious kudzu vine of self that clings and temporarily smothers our yearning to be reconciled to our Father and enter His embrace.

I know all too well how my pride often keeps me from confessing and from changing my behavior. As a graduate counseling intern I met each week with a faculty supervisor to discuss my clients and students. More times than not, the session ended up being about me and how I viewed myself and God, about how I communicated God to these men and women I was privileged to counsel.

During one session, I complained about a particular client who, week after week, sat on my scruffy couch and resisted every attempt on my part to reach his heart. If I pointed out how selfish he was in his marriage, he justified it by recounting how his wife failed him. If I pointed out how selfish he was with me during our short times together, he justified it by pointing out that he didn't know me and therefore couldn't trust me. I felt frustrated because he cut me off at every turn. I wanted him to own his sinful nature.

My supervisor listened attentively and nodded sympathetically as I recounted the latest skirmish. At the end of my narrative, I was hoping for some new strategy or counseling technique to penetrate my client's armor. Instead my supervisor casually asked, "When's the last time you went into your office, shut the door and closed the blinds, and fell face down on the carpet before God? Do you ever feel so weighted with sorrow over your sinfulness that falling down is the only thing you can do?"

I was stunned. My prideful thoughts of better management techniques scattered like marbles. His tone wasn't accusatory, but it felt as if he hadn't been listening to my dilemma. And then his message hit me and stunned me even more. He continued, "I don't think your problem with this client has nearly as much to do with him as it does with you, you and God. I'm not sure you can offer him grace or love as long as you're intent on forcing a confession out of him."

Tears welled up and I knew he spoke the truth. I first had to take the two-by-four out of my own eye before I could even attempt to point out the speck in my brother's. This humbling realization cut through to the core of my competence as a man, a counselor, and a Christian. It cut through all the pretense and self-sufficiency I'd cultivated in most of my daily interactions.

Rather than violate the intimacy I had with God immediately following that session by trying to describe it, let me simply say my confession reminded me of who I am and who God is. It reminded me of why I struggle so with grace, with the perfection of His gift of mercy.

My times with my client suddenly were motivated by something much more powerful and life-changing than my competency as a counselor. How and when he changed no longer depended on my skill or expertise. And honestly, I didn't want it to. I wanted something much more holy and resonant for both of us.

Our hunger for holiness allows us to be convicted by the Holy Spirit when we're in danger of claiming too much ability to achieve holiness on our own. We cannot participate in holy living without Christ. And then our participation amounts to letting go of our own efforts and relying on communication with the Father and His gift of the Holy Spirit to help us live out holiness on a daily basis. We won't be perfect this side of heaven, but we can grow into holy living by deepening our relationship with God through prayer.

Madeleine L'Engle, in her book *Walking on Water*, says: "Our sins defeat us unless we are willing to recognize them, confess them, and so become healed and whole and holy—not qualified, mind you; just holy."[5]

These holy moments of fully appreciating grace are cultivated by prayer.

Eternal Gratitude

Confession causes us to recognize God's grace and holiness, and produces in us an awareness that can't help but make us praise and adore the One who has given Himself to us. Confession leads us to converse even more with our Father and reminds us of what it means to be a living prayer to God—we see Him in His creation by recognizing His signature in the Monets and Chagalls outside our window, in the men and women around us, in the poetry of His Word. Such holy awareness is sustained by the process of confessing our sins before Him as we become aware of them, both sins of commission—the things we do and say—as well as sins of omission—things we don't do or say that we should.

Confession must be a conscious part of our prayer lives. We should not lapse into the presumption of a one-shot conversion mentality that blankets the whole of God's grace over our past, present, and future sins without first owning them. While this is true theologically, such a presumption too easily dismisses the gift. No, we must recognize each day the gift we have been given and our continual need for it. When we view our need of forgiveness and grace the way we view our need for daily food or air underwater, then we taste a daily gratitude that keeps us seeking God's presence instead of fearing it, running from it, dreading it. Such an awareness of our daily need for grace reminds us to constantly converse with our Father.

Questions for Prayer and Reflection

1. What's your greatest barrier to confessing your sins to your Father? What's required? (Consider what you long for more than anything in this world.)

2. Why is humility such an integral part of confession? Read through Psalm 51. Now make a list of the things God does when we confess humbly the way David did in this poem-prayer.

3. Consider the ways you avoid humble confession. Can you recall a time when you avoided facing the consequences of your sin . . . tried to pay for your wrongdoing so you wouldn't have to receive mercy from someone else . . . refused to forgive yourself . . . felt sorry for yourself but didn't really want to change your behavior . . . got mad at someone for catching you . . . or felt unforgivable? What did you learn about yourself and about God from this experience?

4. Read 1 John 1:9. Try to recall a time of humble, heartfelt confession in which you gratefully tasted your Abba's mercy and goodness. How would you describe this experience to a new Christian who doesn't know much about confession?

5. How does a regular time of confession keep the communication channels open with God? Quiet yourself before Him and ask the Spirit to bring to mind sins that continue to block your openness with your Father.

Here in the presence of Almighty God, I kneel in silence,
and with penitent and obedient heart confess my sins,
so that I may obtain forgiveness by your infinite goodness
and mercy.

Most merciful God,
I confess that I have sinned against you
in thought, word, and deed,
by what I have done,

and by what I have left undone.
I have not loved you with my whole heart;
I have not loved my neighbors as myself.
I am truly sorry and I humbly repent.
For the sake of your Son Jesus Christ,
have mercy on me and forgive me;
that I may delight in your will,
and walk in your ways,
to the glory of your Name. Amen.[6]

—BOOK OF COMMON PRAYER

EIGHT

PRAYING FOR RAIN

—

If you pray for rain,
be prepared to deal with some mud.

—ANONYMOUS

In Mark Twain's classic *Huckleberry Finn*, Huck approaches prayer the way many of us do, as an opportunity to ask God for our needs. He tries to learn to pray from Miss Watson and the Widow Douglas, but the results simply aren't consistent. Twain writes:

> Then Miss Watson she took me in the closet and prayed, but nothing came of it. She told me to pray every day, and whatever I asked for I would get it. But it warn't so. I tried it. Once I got a fish-line, but no hooks. It warn't any good to me without hooks. I tried for the hooks three or four times, but somehow I couldn't make it work.

Huck's conclusion is also similar to ours—petitionary prayer doesn't work, at least not the way we want it to:

> I set down, one time, back in the woods, and had a long think about it. I says to myself, if a body can get anything

116

they pray for, why don't Deacon Winn get back the money he lost on pork? Why can't the widow get back her silver snuff-box that was stole? Why can't Miss Watson fat up? No, says I to myself, there ain't nothing to it.[1]

Most of us know what it means to feel the urgency of unpaid bills, a sick child, the grief of a friend, or the desire for a better job. Many of us know what it's like for God to answer some of our prayer requests; we also know the disappointment when He doesn't. Our Father intends both experiences to draw us back to our relationship with Him.

Ask, Seek, Knock

What does it mean to ask God for something? In Chapter Six we examined the Lord's Prayer as a model of the kinds of prayers we should distinguish as our own. We concentrated on three instructive verbs — *give, forgive, deliver.* The Lord's Prayer is a prayer of petition. In a very real sense, so is all of prayer. Even a prayer of gratitude is a request that God accept our thanks. It's no wonder then, that the other half of Jesus' instruction accompanying the Lord's Prayer revolves around asking, seeking, and knocking.

> Then he said, "Imagine what would happen if you went to a friend in the middle of the night and said, 'Friend, lend me three loaves of bread. An old friend traveling through just showed up, and I don't have a thing on hand.'
>
> "The friend answers from his bed, 'Don't bother me. The door's locked; my children are all down for the night; I can't get up to give you anything.'
>
> "But let me tell you, even if he won't get up because he's a friend, if you stand your ground, knocking and waking all the neighbors, he'll finally get up and get you whatever you need.
>
> "Here's what I'm saying:
>
> Ask and you'll get;
> Seek and you'll find;
> Knock and the door will open.

"Don't bargain with God. Be direct. Ask for what you need. This is not a cat-and-mouse, hide-and-seek game we're in. If your little boy asks for a serving of fish, do you scare him with a live snake on his plate? If your little girl asks for an egg, do you trick her with a spider? As bad as you are, you wouldn't think of such a thing—you're at least decent to your own children. And don't you think the Father who conceived you in love will give the Holy Spirit when you ask him?" (Luke 11:5-13, MSG)

As several scholars note, there's an unexpected humor in these examples Jesus uses, a sense of curiosity or irritation that He would even have to explain something as basic as prayer. This reinforces the notion of prayer as something as natural as breathing. At the same time, there's a sense of Jesus thinking that, yes, I do have to explain most things, and even then only some will get it.

Nonetheless, Jesus knew that His instructions on prayer were revolutionary. Although His disciples loved and trusted Him, they still came out of a culture that emphasized the vast chasm between the Holy God and sinful humans. They were used to formal, liturgical prayer with set rules, times, and methods. Jesus' instructions on prayer shook up typical Jewish expectations.

Jesus instructs us to be direct, not to manipulate, bargain, cajole, or make a deal with God (as if we were His equal): "So I say to you: Ask and it will be given to you; seek and you will find; knock and the door will be opened to you" (Luke 11:9). This instruction to ask forthrightly reinforces our direct access to the Father through Jesus. If the Son came to restore our ability to relate intimately to God, then our ability to communicate directly is also restored in the process. This not only undermines the traditional Jewish address of God, it also replaces the need to bargain with God that we often see in the Old Testament. Jacob, Lot, Moses, and Gideon all struck deals with God in various ways. For us today, the ultimate deal has already been completed through the death of Jesus on the cross. We don't have to lay out fleeces, create conditions, sacrifice animals, or barter our labor in order to seek God's favor.

Jesus also informs us that we'll be answered, we'll find, we'll enter in. We're told that all we have to do to get what we want is simply to ask. In fact, Jesus compares our petitions to the Father with a child asking his parent for food. When my Mary Elise asks for a graham cracker, I don't give her a slab of granite from our patio. When she asks for orange juice, I don't give her battery acid. In the same way, our Abba will not give us rocks or acid or snakes or scorpions.

James tells us, "Every good and perfect gift is from above, coming down from the Father of the heavenly lights, who does not change like shifting shadows" (1:17). Bottom line, God is for us more than we can fathom, even when it might not appear that way because we didn't get the particular graham cracker we asked for.

Unanswered Prayers

Why do many of our prayers go unanswered for years, or why are many requests flat-out denied while our lives take apparently opposite turns or tragic undertows that we never prayed for?

This question often causes many of us to view prayer as a futile endeavor. We think: Why should I bother asking when God's going to do what He wants to do anyway? As C. S. Lewis asks, "How is this astonishing promise [of getting what we ask for] to be reconciled (a) with the observed facts? and (b) with the prayer in Gethsemane?"[2] He goes on to elaborate that Jesus, in His omniscience as God, surely knew what had to happen in order for Him to carry out His part in the plan of salvation. Yet in the Garden of Gethsemane Jesus prayed "may this cup be taken from me" (Matthew 26:39). In the end, though, He prayed, as we are instructed elsewhere, "May your will be done" (verse 42).

On the one hand, we are to ask for anything, to be direct with God about our concerns, needs, and desires. On the other hand, we are to temper our requests with seeking God's will rather than our own. This seeming contradiction does not undermine what the Word tells us, but it does create an uncomfortable tension for our prayer lives. We'd all prefer to get what we want when we want it; we want for God's will to be our will. The great writer on prayer, Ole Hallesby, calls this attitude a misuse of petitionary prayer. He says, "As soon as we encounter Him, we immediately look upon Him as another means of gaining our own ends. How can I make use of prayer to the greatest possible advantage for myself?"[3]

It's so easy to be like Huck and discard our petitions when God does not answer them to suit us. Honest petitionary prayer must begin in an examination of our motives. As James instructs us, "When you ask, you do not receive, because you ask with wrong motives, that you may spend what you get on your pleasures" (4:3).

If we discount the purely selfish motives of most of our prayers, at the same time we must accept that we will likely never escape some tint of selfishness in the way we pray. It's part of what it means to be in the process of sanctification—our old nature lingers but does not dictate how we live our lives. So what should we be asking for? What is Jesus saying in this passage about the nature of asking and seeking and knocking?

First, I believe He's telling us we may not get the specific thing—the new bobsled or better job or three-bedroom split-level—we ask for, but we may discover something about why we want it and what it means to us. We'll also learn our response to God if we don't (or do) get it. If we really want God more than the thing we pray for, we may get Him. That is, we may not get the new car or the baby-sitter for Saturday night, but we may move a millimeter closer to knowing God. As Frederick Buechner puts it, "the God you call upon will finally come, and even if he does not bring you the answer you want, he will bring you himself. And maybe at the secret heart of all our prayers that is what we are really praying for."[4]

This desire for God takes me back to my premise, that all prayer is a reflection of our longing for Him. Every request, no matter how selfish or abstract, ambivalent or specific, can be traced back to our deepest yearning for God's presence, our relational desire to bask in His presence like a child on her father's lap. When we ask and seek and knock, we are indeed receiving if we are intent on seeking God more than the request du jour. Jesus concludes, "If you then, though you are evil, know how to give good gifts to your children, how much more will your Father in heaven give the Holy Spirit to those who ask him!" (Luke 11:13). Presumably God gives the Holy Spirit to us when we ask for His presence. However, implicit in Jesus' rhetorical question is the truth that if we really love the Father, the Holy Spirit will by far be the better answer to our petition than the thing we asked for.

There is no guarantee we will receive what we ask for. What is guaranteed is the fulfillment of the deepest need we have—our need for salvation—which enables God to fill our need for Him. Christ died so that we could be on intimate terms with the Father. As Annie Dillard explains,

> "There is not a guarantee in the world. Oh your needs are guaranteed, your needs are absolutely guaranteed by the most stringent of warranties, in the plainest, truest words: knock; seek; ask. But you must read the small print. 'Not as the world giveth, give I unto you.' That's the catch. If you can catch it it will catch you up, aloft, up to any gap at all, and you'll come back, for you will come back, transformed in a way you may not have bargained for—dribbling and crazed."[5]

Second, Jesus is telling us that when we ask, seek, and knock, we are not to give up. We must persist and knock-knock-knock like the peskiest door-to-door salesman. What does this accomplish if not the item requested? After the recalcitrant, sleepy neighbor denies his friend's request at first, Jesus concludes the illustration, "I tell you, though he will not get up and give him the bread because he is his friend, yet because of the man's boldness he will get up and give him as much as he needs" (Luke 11:8).

Power of Persistence

This parallels another parable on prayer in which persistence, once again, seems to be the point:

> He said, "There was once a judge in some city who never gave God a thought and cared nothing for people. A widow in that city kept after him: 'My rights are being violated. Protect me!'
> "He never gave her the time of day. But after this went on and on he said to himself, 'I care nothing what God thinks, even less what people think. But because this widow won't quit badgering me, I'd better do something and see that she gets

justice—otherwise I'm going to end up beaten black-and-blue by her pounding.'"

Then the Master said, "Do you hear what that judge, corrupt as he is, is saying? So what makes you think God won't step in and work justice for his chosen people, who continue to cry out for help? Won't he stick up for them? I assure you, he will. He will not drag his feet. But how much of that kind of persistent faith will the Son of Man find on the earth when he returns?" (Luke 18:2-8, MSG)

A crooked judge doesn't want to give protection to a widow, but he does so because she's such a nag? What does this say about the way we should persevere with our Father?

This seems like we need to become really annoying to God before He'll pay any attention to us. As if somehow we have to compete with three billion other voices from this planet, each clamoring with its urgent request for attention. But that's not what this parable is saying. As with the whole concept of prayer, it is for our benefit not God's that we communicate directly with Him. God knows our needs before we even ask. As Kierkegaard wisely observed, "Prayer does not change God, but changes him who prays."[6] When I must persevere in seeking God I move closer to Him, closer to knowing and living His divine personality rather than loving Him for what He does and can do for me. The first nurtures love, the essence of relationship. The second produces a codependence born of obligation. If we sincerely desire God with all our strength and heart and mind, then persistence in prayer is the only continual love letter we can compose. If we desire His presence more than His presents, then our obedience and loving service reflect our heart's true intent.

Why is this so hard to accept? I believe a lot of it has to do with the way we approach God. Many of us—myself included—often do not want God as much as we want the thing we're praying for. I've prayed for jobs, for children, for books I've wanted to write. I'm blessed with all of those things right now; God has graciously answered many of my prayers. Nonetheless, the gifting of my requests has been according to His timetable, not mine. I prayed for a full-time teaching job last summer and didn't get it. One year later, however, I'm teaching full-time at a different university. I've prayed for a son to complement my beautiful daughters and have not received him yet. Even in answering my prayers, God reminds me of who He is, asking me to trust that His love is so much richer than the measly expressions of it I so often request.

Often we're disappointed even if we get what we pray for. This example is in the realm of "Be careful what you pray for, you might get it." A woman I counseled was in distress over the state of her marriage. Because her husband drank he wasn't able to hold a steady job. Marge prayed and prayed for her husband to get a secure job, something he loved to do, something that would be worth giving up the drink for. Sure enough, an opportunity came his way to be a partner in a small business, a convenience market. He took the job. Marge was ecstatic and knew this was the answer to her prayers. After six weeks, however, her husband, still drinking more than ever, ran off with his new business partner, a woman he'd known from college.

"How cruel God must be," Marge whispered, sitting in my office. "He answered my prayer all right, and then some. Now I don't even have a marriage to pray for. I believe God's punishing me for wanting Tom's sobriety more than His will. Still I know God doesn't want my husband to get drunk, for our marriage to fail. But legally, He answered my prayer for Tom to get a good job. I don't get it."

"Marge," I said, "if I could somehow give you back your marriage to a sober, loving Tom, with only one condition, would you accept it?"

"What condition?"

"That you renounce your faith and never attempt to communicate with God or other Christians ever again."

After pausing she whispered, "No, I couldn't accept that condition. I really do want to love God more than I want my life to be easy. Maybe what I'm learning from this is that my prayer motives are incredibly selfish."

Suffering Our Prayers

So, how do we pray according to God's will? Isn't this just asking Him to do what He's going to do anyway? I believe God asks us to pray according to His will as a sign of trust. Many of us mouth these words, but perhaps we should wait to pray "Thy will be done" until we genuinely mean it. Sometimes we use the words as an "abracadabra" to assure the proper prayer form as we test God, often in the same way we manipulate other people: "If our relationship really means anything to you, then you'll give me 'X'." We become nothing more than petulant teenagers, desperately trying to extort God's goodness as proof of His love for us. Thank Him that He never succumbs to it. Instead He graciously keeps giving Himself through both answered and unanswered prayers.

We pray "Your will be done" as an act of trust, a loving risk of faith. *To pray this way we must be willing to suffer.* We must be willing not to know all of His plan right now; we must be willing to view our unanswered or denied request as an opportunity to trust Him, to love Him for who He is, not for what He does for us.

Once again I recall my niece's death. There's no way I can make sense of the loss from my perspective. My prayers, along with countless others, were not answered the way we wished. It's a loss as empty as the desert. Even if we accept the fact that we're all mortal, we still want to choose the timing of when we and our loved ones die. Instead we're forced to trust that our Father's will is being carried out in a loving harmony that we cannot fully hear right now.

Or consider those nagging sins and habits that dog us for years. Most of us have weak spots that are more susceptible to temptation than others—the love of money, power, sex, food, relationships, and on and on. We pray and pray for them to be taken away. Sometimes they are taken away, but often they are not. We're left to wrestle through our sinful desires to the pure longing at the core of our lives—to know and love our Father. Consider Paul's request to be alleviated from his "thorn in the flesh":

> To keep me from becoming conceited because of these surpassingly great revelations, there was given me a thorn in my flesh, a messenger of Satan, to torment me. Three times I pleaded with the Lord to take it away from me. But he said to me, "My grace is sufficient for you, for my power is made perfect in weakness." That is why, for Christ's sake, I delight in

weaknesses, in insults, in hardships, in persecutions, in difficulties. For when I am weak, then I am strong.
(2 Corinthians 12:7-10)

I find great relief and comfort from Paul's declaration. His maturity provides an example to which I aspire. First, his words make me realize how often I abuse petitionary prayer by always focusing, short-sightedly, on myself and my own pleasure. Second, Paul's words reflect a passion for his Savior, a willingness to trust and joyfully embrace his own weakness because it drives him to his knees in prayer. Paul's thorn reminds him of his human limitations, of his need for God, of his faith that God has a better handle on things than he does.

Paul's words carry a sense of transcendent desperation. They are not a glib, trite, "Oh, well, I guess God knows best!" kind of response while he sneers under his breath. His words reflect a holy acceptance that embraces his weakness because it gives him an opportunity to grow deeper in love with this God who stopped him cold on a road to Damascus.

Annie Dillard, in her sharp and poetic book *Holy the Firm*, describes a similar kind of transcendent desperation at a small, local church she attended:

There is one church here, so I go to it. On Sunday mornings I quit the house and wander down the hill to the white frame church in the firs. On a big Sunday there might be twenty of us there; often I am the only person under sixty, and feel as though I'm on an archaeological tour of Soviet Russia. The members are of mixed denominations; the minister is a Congregationalist, and wears a white shirt. The man knows God. Once, in the middle of the long pastoral prayer of intercession for the whole world—for the gift of wisdom to its leaders, for hope and mercy to the grieving and the pained, succor to the oppressed, and God's grace to all—in the middle of this he stopped, and burst out, "Lord, we bring you these same petitions every week." After a shocked pause, he continued reading the prayer. Because of this I like him very much.[7]

I wonder how often we allow ourselves to express our petitions with such honesty and desperation. We know that God is capable of answering our prayers, both by definition and by personal experience. We must keep asking and growing, seeking and growing, knocking and growing closer and closer to Him whose love for us radiates through the risen Lord Jesus. I believe the lifelong process of petitionary prayer is closely related to what it means for us to work out our salvation with fear and trembling (Philippians 2:12) and to pray without ceasing (1 Thessalonians 5:17). These verses remind us that we will spend our lives longing for God, growing in love with Him, and expressing our desire for Him through our prayers.

When we approach petitionary prayer with this same freedom of expression, our requests seem much more humble, transcendent, and even more direct. An excellent example emerges in Hannah's burning desire for a child. In fact, by examining her story we learn several things about what it means to ask God for our heart's desire.

Asking Honestly

As I read Hannah's story in 1 Samuel, I reflect on the privilege my wife and I have had to get close to at least four couples struggling with infertility. It is a hellish, tormenting desire to want a child and not be able to conceive. Infertile couples endure the doubts, cynicism, drugs, shots, tests, and charts, all for the hope of loving someone. These same emotions burned in Hannah as she longed to bear a child: "In bitterness of soul Hannah wept much and prayed to the LORD" (1:10).

She held nothing back. And then she made a vow, a promise to give her child back to the Lord if He will but give her one. Her vow reveals much about her heart's attitude, both for her Lord and for the object of her petition. I don't believe that making a vow like Hannah's is by any means a guarantee or formula for us to get what we ask for. It's easy to view her vow as a bargaining chip, something most of us have tried before: "If you'll heal me of this disease, Lord, I'll devote my life to missions work" or "Let me marry that special someone, Father, and we'll devote our marriage to serving You." Yet how does this kind of "negotiation" fit with Jesus' instruction to ask the Father directly?

In Hannah's case, she does ask directly and her vow simply reinforces her heart's motive. Similarly for us, it's the motive behind the vow that determines whether we're simply praying out of the desperation of our immediate desire or whether we're agreeing always to remember His gift as a reflection of His will. Hannah allows her desire for a child to be eclipsed by her desire for God's will in her life. "Even if God gives me a child," she implicitly prays, "I'll remember Him first. Loving God remains my priority, not my prayer request."

Such an openness to God's will, sincerely and heart-wrenchingly offered, is likely to be honored, either by His presence and/or by what we're requesting. Hannah realizes what so many of us do not. Asking for any gift from God is really asking to be graced with its stewardship for a short while. Whether He gives us children, finances, ministry, position, status, a good night's sleep, or a fresh tomato, we become stewards of the gift.

Again, as with other modes of prayer, this raises the question of motive. If granted, are we willing to use our gifts for His purposes? Will we—can we—give them back to Him to use through us as He wills? Or is our petition a backhanded way of praying, either consciously or unconsciously, for God to provide us a golden calf, a quick fix that we can justify under the guise of His provision? We are continually called to examine the heart of things, namely ourselves, as we approach our Father with our requests.

Not only are we to take our requests to God, Scripture urges us to share our needs with other people. Hannah did this and received a blessing from the priest Eli. In fact, after sharing her prayer request with him she leaves the temple "no longer downcast" (1 Samuel 1:18). Apart from her prayer concerns, she is comforted and encouraged simply to know that another cares and will lift up her request as well. Other Scriptures reinforce this:

Confess your sins to each other and pray for each other so that you may be healed. The prayer of a righteous man is powerful and effective. (James 5:16)

[For] God . . . is my witness how constantly I remember you in my prayers at all times. (Romans 1:9-10)

Since the day we heard about you, we have not stopped praying for you and asking God to fill you with the knowledge of his will through all spiritual wisdom and understanding. (Colossians 1:9)

We are called to tell our needs to others, to lift them up, to take our eyes off of ourselves and see those around us.

The next thing that strikes me about Hannah's example is her faithfulness. She does her part in facilitating God's answer to her request. After rising early and worshiping the Lord, Hannah and her husband Elkanah make love. True, they might have made love just for the pleasure of it, a joyful response to God for each other. But it's significant that the writer connects these two events so closely. They worship together and then they make love. I see a cause-effect relationship between the two acts. They're willing to do their part after asking God to do His.

So often when couples struggle with infertility, the act of making love hangs over them like a judgment rather than a blessing. Every time their bodies and souls connect yet their egg and sperm do not seems like a taunt, every bit as cruel as the barbs Peninnah (Elkanah's other, fruitful wife) threw at Hannah.

Responding to God's Answer

Hannah faithfully carries out the part of the plan she knows to do and leaves the rest up to God. She doesn't allow her fear of disappointment, potential cynicism, or old angers to hinder her part of the process. She asks God for a child, she makes love to her husband, and trusts God for the outcome, knowing that she might not conceive. It's the same kind of devotion, the same brand of loving faith we see in Abraham and Sarah lying together in their old age, daring to hope they might also conceive a child. It's the same kind of faith, as terrifying as we might find it, that fueled Abraham's trek to the top of Mount Moriah to obediently sacrifice that same son he loved so passionately.

When we truly ask and pray for something, we must back it up in faith by action. Yes, we may be disappointed, but no one has claimed the process is easy. If we truly hope for God through what we ask, as

opposed to hoping for what we ask through God, then we coura-
geously and faithfully do our part.

In Hannah's case, her faithfulness is rewarded. One strong caution:
I don't believe that when our prayers go unanswered we should assume
it's because our faith is not strong enough. Some believers are quick to
claim that God denies requests and doesn't answer others simply
because the askers don't trust Him enough. This is a dangerous judgment for any of us to make about another person. A more loving
response is to persevere with our request and to seek God amidst our
disappointment.

Similarly, we are called to rejoice with one another when God
grants our requests and to remind one another of our stewardship. Our
response after we get our requests often reveals our motives. Hannah
gratefully names her son Samuel "because I asked the LORD for him"
(1 Samuel 1:20). The name is a constant reminder of God's answer to
her request. And perhaps the most telling part of all, Hannah makes
good on her vow with a joyful heart. In her place, I might hem and haw
and try to wheedle out of my vow. I would cling to my child and beg
to keep him as long as I could; my reluctance would betray my motives
from the very first. I'd cry that's unfair and beg the Lord not to take back
this gift of His.

Not Hannah. She not only takes her newly weaned son to the
temple and turns him over to Eli, she then prays one of the most exul-
tant songs of thanksgiving recorded in Scripture. "There is no one holy
like the LORD," she sings, "there is no one besides you." (1 Samuel 2:2)
Her heart is full. She asks, receives, and gives back. I believe this is a
good motive-tester for our own requests: Are we willing to give what
He gifts us back to Him, either through its use or whenever He wants
it back?

We must seek the Lord with all our hearts, despite the gifts He gives
or withholds. Such is the essence of true petitionary prayer. We are to
ask, seek, and knock, trusting that the best gift of all is who He is and
how He reveals Himself amidst our asking and seeking. True petitionary prayer waits for the Lord to reveal Himself. It is the essence of
love, an interchange between parent and child, a request between lover
and beloved.

Questions for Prayer and Reflection

1. What has been your experience with asking God for things? Try to recall both times when He's granted your requests as well as times when He hasn't. What kinds of things do you ask Him for?

2. Make a list of everything you earnestly long for before the Lord. Examine your motives without discounting something because it seems selfish, but acknowledge that before your Father as well.

3. Seek out someone to pray for this week—someone you might not normally pursue—and ask what you can pray for them. If they are receptive, share one of your personal requests. If it's feasible, you may want to pray together.

4. What do you yearn for in your petitions to God? How often do you really yearn for Him rather than for what He can do for you? How often are you willing to trust that our needs are "guaranteed, but not as the world giveth," as Annie Dillard puts it? How does this make you feel—comforted, confused, angry, uncomfortable, relieved?

5. Consider the prayer of Teresa of Avila: "From silly devotions and from sour-faced saints, good Lord, deliver us."[8] What's she really asking for in this prayer? What distractions to a deeper prayer life would you ask God to remove from your life?

Grant me, O Lord, heavenly wisdom,
that I may learn to seek you above all things,
and to understand all other things as they are
according to the order of your wisdom. Amen.[9]

—Thomas à Kempis

PIED BEAUTY

Glory be to God for dappled things—
For skies of couple-colour as a brinded cow;
For rose-moles all in stipple upon trout that swim;
Fresh-firecoal chestnut-falls; finches' wings;
Landscape plotted and pieced—fold, fallow, and plough;
And all trades, their gear and tackle and trim.

All things counter, original, spare, strange;
Whatever is fickle, freckled (who knows how?)
With swift, slow; sweet, sour; adazzle, dim;
He fathers-forth whose beauty is past change:
Praise him.

—GERARD MANLEY HOPKINS

I am wheeling the trash cans from the curb back to my garage on this late May evening. The cool blue sun dismantles itself with golden perfection along the foothills west of me. I stop because the neighbor's lone aspen across the street trembles with wind moist from the high country. Since moving to Colorado, I have watched aspens shimmy like spangled dancers, new green now, with gold six months away, and I am still not used to it. Trees do not do this in Tennessee where I grew up. The aspens have bark pale as my daughter's wrist in winter, washed just gray enough for us to notice. They are narrow-waisted and cannot help noticing themselves.

This particular evening I am re-collecting myself and my trash cans and I'm cooled by each green spade-shaped leaf as it fans itself on this twelve-foot pole. Sunlight blinds me in a final spill, an old-time photographer's magnesium flash, poof!, and the moment stops. The silence reminds me of a play in which the lights dim except for the spotlight on the actor who steps forward and talks to us like he knows we've been watching the whole time. Spring has been wet and slow to unpack itself this year. Something inside me trembles with the tree before I move on and replace the hefty cans on the smooth cement inside my garage. This spring evening became a living psalm.

Eruptions of Praise

In such moments something holy spills out of me, something not of myself, but natural nonetheless. It is a joyous eruption that feels as right as rain, as unpredictable as a volcano. I'm created for this. I feel what Gerard Manley Hopkins must have felt when he noticed the "dappled things" that simply delighted him: the black-and-white cow spots, the rainbow moles on a trout's belly, the color of a finch's wings. These are moments we are all called to, and larger ones, still.

At times we enounter praiseful moments in which we take the time to notice the small details of God's essence in the natural world, in the experiences of our lives, or in our response to His written or spoken Word. We're left with a tearful "thank you" that has nothing to do with us and everything to do with being privileged to witness that moment at a daughter's birthday party or the way the light enveloped the contour of a friend's face or the way the wind blew an aspen tree. It is the responsive thrill of being loved beyond what we can contain in this lifetime.

In such beautiful, timeless moments it is not difficult to be a kind of living prayer. It makes sense to "be joyful always; pray continually; give thanks in all circumstances" and to recognize that "this is God's will for you in Christ Jesus" (1 Thessalonians 5:16-18). These moments don't just happen. I believe they are cultivated. Perhaps they come naturally to begin with—something as simple as children marveling at the breath of the wind lifting a dandelion. But we get older, and it takes more and more to impress us, to awe us, to still us in our tracks. And then most of us begin trying to make such awe-inspiring moments happen for ourselves. We seek out pleasure for its own sake as a way of taking us out of all the painful, tedious days that life often amounts to.

At some point, usually when we invite Christ into our lives, we let go of crafting our idols, of seeking pleasure as an end in itself. Through the Holy Spirit we return to a simplicity of faith that enables us to give thanks for all things, not just the things we like or find beautiful. We become mature enough to trust that even though we may not feel like giving thanks, God is still in charge of something much larger and grander than we can imagine. To live a prayerful, hopeful life of gratitude means that we trust with childlike faith our Father who loves us beyond our worst acts or thoughts. To live a prayer-centered life of gratitude means cultivating a childlike awareness of the world around us and praising Him.

We do this by looking for God every day. We cultivate an awareness of His creation by staying tuned to the world around us. We don't take for granted that our car is running well. We notice the three children waiting at the bus stop and wave to them. The weather becomes a reminder of God's beauty as well as His power. We surprise others with a bouquet of daisies or an ice-cream cone. We take our eyes off ourselves and look at the people around us, the landscape around us, and the divine moments of pied beauty. It means that we also grieve the absence of beauty, peace, and God's presence. We enter into the fragments of this fallen world and hope the ultimate hope—the world's redemption through the power and kindness of God's gift of Jesus.

In this way we learn to give thanks for all things. Adoration reflects this childlike gratitude. The Father created us to adore Him. Everything from the *New England Primer's* catechism—"What is the chief aim of man? To glorify God and enjoy Him forever"—to the Psalms—"My heart is steadfast, O God; I will sing and make music with all my soul" (108:1)—to our individual experiences testify to this aspect of our being. Scripture is consistently clear about this: We are created to worship God (see Exodus 34:12-16; Isaiah 45:23; Romans 14:11). This longing to worship, to be caught up in something larger and transcendent than ourselves, is the same longing that leads us to idolatry when we are unwilling to bow before our Lord. The practice of adoration, on the other hand, fulfills us at our deepest level as we connect ourselves in awe and wonder to our Abba Father, His glorious Son, and the burning Spirit of love.

The mystics, a group of medieval believers who actively pursued the mystery of knowing and loving God, beautifully express this longing. Saint Anselm wrote, "Lord Jesus Christ, let me seek you by desiring you, and let me desire you by seeking you; let me find you by loving you, and love you in finding you."[1] Or "Blessed be thou for ever, let all things praise thee. May thy name be for ever glorified" as Teresa of Avila wrote.[2]

Grateful Living

We adore God in two ways—when we thank our Father for the things He does for us, the gifts He gives us daily, and when we praise Him simply because of who He is. Most scholars and teachers indicate the latter to be a purer kind of adoration since it is less self-centered and doesn't rely on our personal circumstances. However, as some have pointed out, most recently Richard Foster, "the two weave themselves in and out of one another and become part of an organic whole."[3] He goes on to note the way biblical authors so often use thanksgiving and praise interchangeably, especially in the Psalms.

It's difficult to separate our knowledge of God from our experience of Him. We can use language to describe Him all we want, but when we experience His goodness, mercy, love, and kindness, we suddenly have a richer context for what the words mean. It's easy to say, "God refreshes us," but to experience the feel of a brisk waterfall on a hot July afternoon gives us experience to go with our praise. Of course our experiences and comparisons, no matter how much we imagine them magnified, can never truly capture the majesty of our King. But we are called to a joyful pursuit of grateful living as we grow in loving awareness of our Father.

When we are grieved by the weight of our sin and yearn for Him who is without fault or blemish, then we begin to experience the humility needed to taste true gratitude. This is why confession is such an integral part of the prayerful, ongoing journey of the Christian life. When we consider God's holiness, when we see it or experience it, we are moved, like Isaiah, to recognize how unclean we are.

Isaiah glimpses the Holy One, surrounded by His guarding seraphim, "high and exalted, and the train of his robe filled the temple" (6:1). Isaiah immediately cries, "Woe to me! I am ruined! For I am a man of unclean lips, and I live among a people of unclean lips, and my eyes have seen the King, the LORD Almighty" (6:5). One of the angels then seizes a burning coal from the altar and places it on Isaiah's mouth, saying, "See, this has touched your lips; your guilt is taken away and your sin atoned for" (6:7).

When we earnestly seek adoration as a way to glimpse the holiness of God—His goodness and righteousness and perfection—then I believe we have little choice except to recognize how unworthy, unholy, un-good, and un-perfect we are by comparison. Such a contrast can humble us and lead us to seek God's merciful forgiveness, to ask for more of the burning coal of Christ's sacrificial love that cleanses our iniquity. It is nothing but grace, then, to taste the goodness of His mercy to us—imagine being in the driest desert and tasting the sweetest, coldest wild strawberries—through the gift of Jesus' intervention on our behalf. The unexpectedness of it is as much a part of the gift as the undeservedness. Such is grace.

How do we sing our prayer in response to such grace? The best example I can think of is the woman who washed Jesus' feet with her tears and anointed them with costly perfume. Imagine yourself in this scene and think about what it reveals of forgiveness and gratitude.

One of the Pharisees asked him over for a meal. He went to the Pharisee's house and sat down at the dinner table. Just then a woman of the village, the town harlot, having learned that Jesus was a guest in the home of the Pharisee, came with a bottle of very expensive perfume and stood at his feet, weeping, raining tears on his feet. Letting down her hair, she dried his feet, kissed them, and anointed them with the perfume. When the Pharisee who had invited him saw this, he said to himself, "If this man was the prophet I thought he was, he would have known what kind of woman this is who is falling all over him."

Jesus said to him, "Simon, I have something to tell you."

"Oh? Tell me."

"Two men were in debt to a banker. One owed five hundred silver pieces, the other fifty. Neither of them could pay up, and so the banker canceled both debts. Which of the two would be more grateful?"

Simon answered, "I suppose the one who was forgiven the most."

"That's right," said Jesus. Then turning to the woman, but speaking to Simon, he said, "Do you see this woman? I came to your home; you provided no water for my feet, but she rained tears on my feet and dried them with her hair. You gave me no greeting, but from the time I arrived she hasn't quit kissing my feet. You provided nothing for freshening up, but she has soothed my feet with perfume. Impressive, isn't it? She was for-given many, many sins, and so she is very, very grateful. If the forgiveness is minimal, the gratitude is minimal."

Then he spoke to her: "I forgive your sins."

That set the dinner guests talking behind his back: "Who does he think he is, forgiving sins!"

He ignored them and said to the woman, "Your faith has saved you. Go in peace." (Luke 7:36-50, MSG)

Debt of Thanks

On one hand the story is simple and direct. Jesus makes His point with a comparison that still speaks to the heart of what we so often consider important: money. The story illustrates the difference between owing money that can't be repaid in a lifetime of hard work and owing a day's salary. Both debts are miraculously paid or canceled. The fresh air of being debt free infuses our spirits with exhilaration, with gratitude beyond reckoning. There's a universal motivation to confess because we know the character of our loving Father. "He who conceals his sins does not prosper, but whoever confesses and renounces them finds mercy" (Proverbs 28:13).

On the other hand, the story is awash with the depth of this par-ticular woman's gratitude, with the joy that comes from getting her life back. Both her sinful lifestyle, most likely prostitution, and her offer-ing of gratitude are intensely personal. It's hard to imagine a more inti-mate sin than exchanging one's body, one's sexuality, with a stranger for money. To be a successful prostitute (or idolater, which we all are), she had to deaden her soul to the numbing power of sin. When she came alive to the hope of forgiveness, she had to face the wrongness of her transgression, not justify or explain it or deny it. She realized her sin's grievous impact on her relationship with God.

The woman breaks into tears. The only thing she can even imagine offering is even more intimate than selling her body. She literally presents herself as a "living and holy sacrifice" (Romans 12:1, NASB) before her Lord and Redeemer. The same should be true for us. Our gratitude should move us to offer ourselves to God. It's the only response we can muster in light of truly tasting the goodness of God's mercy. We must say with Teresa of Avila, "Here is my life; here is my honour and my will. I have given it all to thee; I am thine; dispose of me according to thy desire."[4]

What keeps us from embracing this kind of grace and living out such a perfumed life of gratitude? The same old selfishness God saved us from the first time, once and for all. It continues to quiver and jerk with the rigor mortis of passing away, reluctant to make room for the new heart transplanted within us through the indwelling Christ, through the power of the Holy Spirit breathing new life in and through us. This is the tension of the Christian life, the process of sanctification.

We need grace on a daily basis. That's why it's so important to confess, to get up from our falls, and to be reminded of who we are in Christ, of who our Father is. That's why it's so important to live out our gratitude. The apostle Peter expresses this kind of attitude:

> What a God we have! And how fortunate we are to have him, this Father of our Master Jesus! Because Jesus was raised from the dead, we've been given a brand-new life and have everything to live for, including a future in heaven—and the future starts now! God is keeping careful watch over us and the future. The Day is coming when you'll have it all—life healed and whole.
>
> I know how great this makes you feel, even though you have to put up with every kind of aggravation in the meantime. Pure gold put in the fire comes out of it *proved* pure; genuine faith put through this suffering comes out *proved* genuine. When Jesus wraps this all up, it's your faith, not your gold, that God will have on display as evidence of his victory.
>
> You never saw him, yet you love him. You still don't see him, yet you trust him— with laughter and singing. Because you kept on believing, you'll get what you're looking forward to, total salvation. (1 Peter 1:3-9, MSG)

Two things strike me about this passage. First, Peter, of all people, wrote it. This is the same Peter who sincerely pledged his love to Jesus but then found himself denying even knowing Him a few hours later. In fact, Peter denied Jesus not once but three times. The weight of Peter's shame and sorrow could easily have derailed his love for Jesus and his ministry. But Peter knew Jesus loved him despite his failure.

After Jesus' crucifixion and resurrection, He appears beachside, preparing breakfast for the apostles as they come in from fishing. When Peter recognizes his Master, he dives into the water and swims ashore. He's not reluctant to face the Lord, even though he betrayed Him. Peter knows Jesus' loving character. Peter goes on to live out his gratitude for the rest of his life. As we experience the forgiveness of Christ, we are called to do the same.

Hope and Praise

The other point I notice in this passage is how critical hope is to our ability to live a prayer-centered life. Hope springs from a deep appreciation for what God has done in our lives through Christ. But hope exudes an even greater anticipation of what is still to be done, both in us and in the world. In hope, we long to be with Him, to see His face, to hear His voice. Hope motivates our faith and deepens our anticipation of fulfillment with a richness our jubilant glimpses here only tease us.

In fact, nowhere does hope and prayer converge more naturally than in the language of praise.

> I waited patiently for the LORD,
>> he turned to me and heard my cry.
> He lifted me out of the slimy pit,
>> out of the mud and mire;
> he set my feet on a rock
>> and gave me a firm place to stand.
> He put a *new song* in my mouth,
>> *a hymn of praise* to our God. (Psalm 40:1-3, emphasis added)

> I would have despaired unless I had believed that I
>> would see the goodness of the LORD

in the land of the living.
Wait for the LORD;
be strong, and let your heart take courage;
Yes, wait for the LORD. (Psalm 27:13-14, NASB)

Even in the midst of melancholy, in lamenting psalms, praise emerges in a hopeful spurt. "How long, O LORD? Will you forget me forever?" begins this psalm, which then concludes, "But I trust in your unfailing love; my heart rejoices in your salvation. I will sing to the LORD, for he has been good to me" (Psalm 13:1,5-6).

We would all do well to learn from this kind of prayer-psalm in which the pray-er embraces the tension of living amidst the painful realities of life while still believing in the bountiful hope of eternity. This kind of prayer crystallizes what it means to give thanks in all things without living in denial that life is hard or without diminishing our hope in God's love and sovereignty.

In fact, the Psalter as a whole, according to Old Testament scholar Brevard Childs contains a predominant eschatological theme: "Even when the psalmist turns briefly to reflect on the past in praise of the 'great things that Yahweh has done,' [126:3] invariably the movement shifts and again the hope of salvation is projected into the future."[5] This is reinforced by Eugene Peterson who asserts that all prayers, like all psalms, are not just about our future hope but become expressions of praise.

> The Psalms show praise as the end of prayer in both meanings of the word: the terminus, the last word in the final Psalm 150; and the goal at which all the psalm-prayers arrive after their long travels throughout the unmapped back countries of pain, doubt, and trouble, with only occasional vistas of the sunlit lands, along the way. All prayer, pursued far enough, becomes praise. Any prayer, no matter how desperate its origin, no matter how angry and fearful the experiences it traverses, ends up in praise.[6]

If each and every prayer is indeed a yearning sigh to God, then it ultimately carries with it some fundamental melody of praise, despite

the dissonance of a counter melody. Why release our complaints, sad-
nesses, joys, and sorrows to God, if somewhere underneath them we
don't believe and dare to hope that He cares about us, cares about every
one of our dead sparrow kind of days (Matthew 10:29)?

The deeper we grow in loving God, the deeper our praise and
thanksgiving. Like the tenth leper who returned to thank our Lord
(Luke 17:11-19), we can't help but return to the source of our life-sav-
ing encounter and lovingly serve Him.

For us, returning in thanks means that we remember God's part in
our joy and praise Him for it. All our biblical examples point to this
process of responding to grace by remembering the contrast between the
old life and the new, then thanking God and changing the way they live.
Hannah . . . the woman who washed Jesus' feet . . . Peter . . . the tenth
leper—all returned to the source of their gratitude and then proceeded
to serve God out of it.

Avoiding Spiritual Amnesia

While it sounds simple to live out of gratitude for what God does for us,
we often experience spiritual amnesia. In the heat of temptation, when
life circumstances get tough, even when things are going well, we easily forget what God has done for us. Time and again we see the nation
of Israel forget how God has delivered them from other nations, as well
as their own fickleness. Yahweh pursues them and exhorts them to
remember in order to live.

How can we remember God's grace in our lives? One way is to collect symbols and songs, momentos and spiritual souvenirs that represent our richest moments with Him. For me, one hymn blends the kind
of gratitude I'm talking about with such honest, yet poetic, finesse that
I don't know how to describe it any better.

Come, Thou Fount of every blessing,
Tune my heart to sing Thy grace;
Streams of mercy, never ceasing,
Call for songs of loudest praise.
Teach me some melodious sonnet,
Sung by flaming tongues above;

Praise His name—I'm fixed upon it—
Name of God's redeeming love.

Hitherto Thy love has blest me;
Thou hast brought me to this place;
And I know Thy hand will bring me
Safely home by Thy good grace.
Jesus sought me when a stranger,
Wandering from the fold of God;
He, to rescue me from danger,
Bought me with His precious blood.

O to grace how great a debtor
Daily I'm constrained to be!
Let Thy goodness, like a fetter,
Bind my wandering heart to Thee:
Prone to wander, Lord I feel it,
Prone to leave the God I love;
Here's my heart, O take and seal it,
Seal it for Thy courts above.[7]

This hymn captures both our longing for more of God and the fickleness of our hearts. The hymn's author, Robert Robinson, experienced grace dramatically, having lived a gang lifestyle in London in the mid-1700s. He ridiculed believers, and one night he dropped in on a service being conducted by George Whitefield to mock those attending. He was so taken aback by God's overwhelming love that he not only became a believer, but a minister, scholar, and hymn writer.[8]

The hymn "Come Thou Fount" also means a great deal to me because my wife, knowing it was my favorite hymn, had it calligraphied and framed, and she surprised me with it for my birthday years ago. It reminds me of what a gift she is, unexpected and grace-bearing, given to me by my Father. It burns in me a desire to gift her with the same kind of love.

Every morning when I get up, my eyes wade across this green-matted verse and remind me of what it means to live a life of thanks. I know a little of what Robinson must have felt when he penned it.

This kind of gratitude accretes over our lifetime. It loses more of itself in the love of our Lord until, as Annie Dillard puts it, we "pray at the last not 'please,' but 'thank you,' as a guest thanks his host at the door."[9] Our lives become living poems of praise, tapestries that manifest a pattern of thanks throughout the cloth. It is no wonder then, that Dillard concludes her book *Pilgrim at Tinker Creek* by proclaiming:

> Divinity is not playful. The universe was not made in jest
> but in solemn incomprehensible earnest. By a power that is
> unfathomably secret, and holy, and fleet. There is nothing to
> be done about it, but ignore it, or see. . . . And like Billy
> Bray I go my way, and my left foot says, "Glory," and my
> right foot says, "Amen" in and out of Shadow Creek,
> upstream and down, exultant, in a daze, dancing, to the
> twin silver trumpets of praise.[10]

And how will we live out our faith? With struggles? Surely. With seasons of doubt and anger, betrayal and fear? Of course. But we are called to live out our days as living psalms, the poems of God's handiwork, noticing the sobering beauty of a lone aspen tree, or hearing the voice of God on the wind. We're called to seek with hungry hearts the Word of God that lives and breathes and speaks to us still.

When we pray and give thanks and praise, we are closer to the center of the universe than we can imagine. It is the appetizer of desire that stirs the essence of our lonely souls. It is the essence of praise.

Questions for Prayer and Reflection

1. Describe the most recent moment when you paused during your day to notice some detail of God's presence in your life. How did you respond?

2. What do you feel as you read the story of the prostitute who washed Jesus' feet with her tears and perfumed them with rare oils? What act of gratitude have you felt prompted to perform in the past? What gift of self might the Spirit be prompting you to give now? Prayerfully seek His direction on how to give with a grateful heart.

3. What keeps you from living a life fueled by gratitude for what God has done for you? Write down your thoughts. What would it mean for you to embrace what you long for and know to be true about your relationship with God?

4. Read Psalm 145. Personalize it by writing your own version or choose another of the praise psalms to personalize. You don't have to write in "biblical" language; just keep your words honest and heartfelt. If you're going through a difficult time right now, you might want to model your psalm more after Psalm 13. You can share your present painful feelings or circumstances and still choose to praise God.

5. What hymns or pieces of music prompt you to praise and thanks-giving? Make a special effort this week to listen to an old favorite as well as seek out new music that moves you to worship.

———

Though our mouths were full of song as the sea,
Our tongues of exultation as the fullness of its waves,
And our lips of praise as the plains of the firmament:
Though our eyes gave light as the sun and moon:
Though our hands were outspread as the eagles of heaven;
And our feet were swift as hinds,

Yet should we be unable to thank Thee,
O Lord our God and God of our fathers,
And to bless Thy Name for even one of the countless
     thousands
And tens of thousands
Of kindnesses which Thou hast done by our fathers
     and by us. [11]

—Jewish Prayer from the Service of the Orthodox Synagogue
for the Festival of Tabernacles

PART FOUR

RESTLESS PEACE: FRUITS OF PRAYER

—

Sometimes I ride a bucking faith
while one hand grips and the other flails the air,
and like any daredevil I gouge with my heels for blood,
for a wilder ride, for more.

—ANNIE DILLARD, PILGRIM AT TINKER CREEK

—

Our lives must be holy as our prayers.
Our prayers are to prove their reality
by the fruit they bear in the holiness or our life.
True devotion in prayer will assuredly be rewarded,
by God's grace, with the power to live a life of true devotion
to Him and His service.

— ANDREW MURRAY

—

Peace I leave with you;
My peace I give to you;
not as the world gives, do I give to you.
⌈Let not your heart be troubled, nor let it be fearful. ⌉

—JOHN 14:27 (NASB)

LIVING
OUR PRAYERS

———

Prayer is not a preparation for work
or an indispensable condition for effective ministry.
Prayer is life; prayer and ministry are the same
and can never be divorced.[1]

—HENRI NOUWEN

Many of my friends inspire me in the way they live out their faith. Eric, for example, works at an inner-city youth center, tutoring kids with their homework and then playing basketball or Ping-Pong with them. He also lives about two blocks from the center, located in a gang-infested part of town. He doesn't have to live there; his family's wealth could easily provide him with his own house in the better parts of Denver. But Eric tells me he likes living close to the boys and girls he cares for. He wants them to know he doesn't view them as a service project; he doesn't commute from a sheltered suburban life and offer his time so that he can feel good about himself. He's one of them. We're all one of them, he says.

My friend Pam runs a food bank in a rural area of the South. She has several college degrees and pursued counseling for a while, but finally decided she could do more good by feeding people's bellies before their souls. She explains, "It's hard scrounging up support from businesses and churches, but I always think about Jesus saying, 'For I was hungry and you gave me something to eat, thirsty and you gave me something to drink, I was a stranger and you invited me in' (Matthew 25:35). This is the way Jesus cared for people. He met their physical needs in order to reveal their spiritual needs. He gave them bread before He gave them the Bread of Life."

Finally, there's Liz who counsels people with chronic mental illness in downtown Denver. She works with many welfare moms, women with sad stories and hard struggles ahead. "Why do you do it?" I asked. "What keeps you going?"

"There's a quiet desperation in most of the women's eyes I counsel," she replied. "They want to believe in something better, but there's not much to offer them hope. I want to be one small part of offering them hope. I know what it's like to be in their place—I grew up that way. What keeps me going? I pray a lot. I pray for patience and for love."

We don't all have to go to the inner city, the food bank, or the counseling center to find people who need His love. But Eric, Pam, and Liz inspire me because they seek to be Jesus to other people, and they're honest about how hard it can be to serve the way they feel called to serve. All three of them agree with Liz's response that prayer sustains them and their ministry to others.

"Without prayer," Eric said, "I'd have given up on these kids a long time ago. Praying for them makes me realize that hope is a process. Ministry comes from the way I live 24 hours a day, 7 days a week, not just an hour now and then."

The Power Source of Prayer

Perhaps we can't relate to their specific ministries, but if we've experienced the love of Christ, then we all know what it means to want to pass on that love to others. How we do that becomes our ministry. As Eric said, service and ministry are not occasional parts of the Christian life. How we live every day reflects our willingness to serve. The only way any of us can do this is the combining of our willingness and God's supernatural power. The way we do this is by following Jesus' example.

The fuel for Jesus' ministry was love. The conduit for accessing the power source of His Father's love was prayer. This combination enabled Him to transcend the limits of human emotions, circumstantial barriers, the demands of His followers, and the antagonism of the Jewish officials. Jesus' love for the Father and His constant communication with Him focused His ministry with clarity, simplicity, and power.

Let's consider an example. After the death of John the Baptizer, Jesus retreats "to a lonely place by Himself" (Matthew 14:13, NASB). The multitudes follow Him and clamor for His attention. Jesus feels compassion for them and heals the sick (14:14). As the afternoon shadows gather, the disciples tell Jesus to send the crowds away for dinner.

> But Jesus said to them, "They do not need to go away; you give them something to eat!" And they said to Him, "We have here only five loaves and two fish." And He said, "Bring them here to Me." And ordering the multitudes to recline on the grass, He took the five loaves and the two fish, and looking up toward heaven, He blessed the food, and breaking the loaves He gave them to the disciples, and the disciples gave to the multitudes, and they all ate, and were satisfied. And they picked up what was left over of the broken pieces, twelve full baskets. And there were about five thousand men who ate, aside from women and children.
>
> And immediately He made the disciples get into the boat, and go ahead of Him to the other side, while He sent the multitudes away. And after He had sent the multitudes away, He went up to the mountain by Himself to pray; and when it was evening, He was there alone. (Matthew 14:16-23, NASB)

Selfless Service

In this story we see Jesus at the height of His ministry of healing, teaching, and feeding thousands of eager, curious Jews. Notice that in this episode of His life Jesus faces a full range of emotions—from grief at John's death to compassion for the crowds that can't leave Him alone; from generosity as the ultimate host to the lonely solitude after the crowd has gone.

In the midst of grief most of us are reluctant to give ourselves so graciously to those who need us. We feel entitled to our private sorrow, often justifiably so. Nevertheless, we see our Lord give despite His feelings, perhaps despite His own need of time alone. Rather than showing annoyance or anger at the people who tracked Him from the city, He feels compassion and heals them.

Next, notice that Jesus willingly serves those around Him. The disciples do their best to think ahead. "Send them away before supper time!" they say. But Jesus puts the burden of the next meal back on the disciples, who complain that they simply don't have enough food. Jesus proceeds to bless the meal and distribute it. He does what can be done at the moment and provides service on a moment-by-moment basis, thinking of others before Himself. Even after the meal is over, Jesus sends the disciples away first, then the multitudes, then He allows Himself more time alone.

Circumstances are not always the barrier they appear to be, especially if we take our cue from the Master, who was the greatest servant, lovingly giving of Himself to those in need. We, too, must learn to sacrifice ourselves and our emotions. Yes, we must spend time alone, and we should avoid ministry burnout, but the way we do that is through prayer.

How did Jesus overcome His emotions and the limits of circumstance? He stayed in constant communion with His Abba Father. While Jesus certainly had supernatural resources to draw upon as the Son of God, He was also a human being like you and me. He was tired. He was sad. There didn't seem to be enough food. What sustained Him? Prayer—the anchor of His ministry. Jesus bathed Himself and His gifts to those around Him in prayer. In a lonely place by Himself, Jesus shared His grief with His Father. Under pressure to provide a meal for thousands of hungry followers, Jesus looked toward heaven and gave thanks. After the crowd departed, when He was alone once again, Jesus went up on a mountainside to pray. His life and His ministry were one and the same. He talked with His Father about everything He felt and everything He did. Jesus' prayers were not merely demands for provision or a ritualistic prelude, they reinforced His relationship with the Father. He called home before heading to the battlefront.

Unlike our distinction between "real life" and ministry, Jesus modeled a life yielded in service and reinforced by the intimacy of prayer. At each crisis or turning point in His life, our Lord prayed and refreshed Himself in His Father's love, wisdom, guidance, and freedom. As writer and teacher Brennan Manning observes, "A central theme in the personal life of Jesus Christ, which lies at the very heart of the revelation that He is, is His growing intimacy with, trust in, and love of His Abba."[2]

Examination of other key points in His ministry bears this out. Jesus renews Himself through prayer right before He chooses His disciples for ministry: "And it was at this time that He went off to the mountain to pray, and He spent the whole night in prayer to God" (Luke 6:12, NASB). He did the same when the multitudes of people were about to crown Him king and recognize Him as the One foretold by prophets, a threshold of success many of us would have eagerly embraced in His place. Instead, He retreats. "Jesus, knowing that they intended to come and make him king by force, withdrew again to a mountain by himself" (John 6:15). Intimacy with the Father was more important than any title, wealth, or crown other people could bestow.

This pattern continues. In the midst of preaching before multitudes, performing miracles, and healing, Jesus continually drenched His ministry in prayerful discourse with His Father. Consider the most pivotal moments of all, right before one of His own betrayed and handed Him over to the Jewish leaders to be crucified, and as He hangs on the cross between two thieves. In Gethsemane, He prays a very human prayer by asking that "this cup might pass." C. S. Lewis explains, "The prayer in Gethsemane shows that the preceding anxiety is equally God's will and equally part of our human destiny. The perfect Man experienced it. And the servant is not greater than the master."[3]

Christ embodied and embraced the tension to which we are all called, to express our most honest selves and to trust in the One who knows us deeper than we know ourselves. Despite the grueling anguish Jesus had already faced, and the torture before Him, He still was willing to trust, yield, and obey. Why? Because He was living out what it meant to be loved with an intensity and purity that overwhelms and undergirds.

From prayerful intimacy with His Father, Jesus learned more of God's character as well as His own identity. As a boy, Christ lived in conversation with His Dad and consequently grew in strength, wisdom, and the grace of God (Luke 2:40). As the "beloved Son, in whom I am well-pleased" (Matthew 3:17, NASB), Jesus continued to experience the warmth and security of God's blessed presence. In fact, His awareness of His identity is so central to His ministry that Satan attacks it in an attempt to undermine His ministry.

Recall after His baptism by John (Matthew 3:13-17), before He begins His public ministry, Jesus retreats to the desert for prayer and fasting. This sets the stage for His confrontation with the Tempter, who tries to undermine Jesus' *relationship* with God the Father (Matthew 4:1-11). He tempts Jesus physically ("Turn these stones to bread"), emotionally ("If you're really God's Son, then jump!"), and spiritually ("Worship me and the kingdoms of the world are Yours"). Jesus resists these multiple attacks on His identity because He knows who He is. His replies reflect this awareness: "It takes more than bread to stay alive. It takes a steady stream of words from God's mouth. Don't test the Lord your God. Worship the Lord your God, and only Him. Serve Him with absolute single-heartedness."[4]

In fact, Satan attacks our identity, our relationship with God, with every temptation he proffers. Too often, temptation and spiritual warfare are seen as more of a chess match than a relational drama. The Enemy would have us think this, for if we feel more like pawns than beloved children of our King, we'll succumb more easily. The remedy is continual, prayerful communication with the Father about our weaknesses, our longings, and our service to others. The remedy is to immerse ourselves in the cool, crystal stream of His love.

Passion Fruits of Prayer

Even with metal spikes puncturing His body and the hot, slow waltz of blood trickling down, Jesus prays from this place of honest intimacy. "My God, my God, why have you forsaken me?" (Matthew 27:46). He does not ask, "Why am I having to go through such humiliation and pain?" but rather, "Where are you?"—a wail of lost love. As many scholars explain, this is the hardest moment for both Father and Son. At this point God had to separate Himself from His most Beloved in order for the Law to be broken and the sacrifice to be complete. It is at this moment that Jesus is most human and, mysteriously, most perfectly divine, the only One capable of taking on what we deserved.

Why did Christ do this? Only love could enable Him to give Himself so selflessly for us who did not deserve it. But that's the essence of grace—a demonstration of love that is not logical, reasonable, or explicable. God gave up His most beloved Son because He so loved us (John 3:16). Jesus gave up His life because He experiences the Father's love. He loves us because God loves us and He loves God.

Jesus declared, "I am the vine; you are the branches. If a man remains in me and I in him, he will bear much fruit; apart from me you can do nothing. . . . As the Father has loved me, so have I loved you. Now remain in my love" (John 15:5,9). Only love motivates the Father to relinquish His most beloved Son into a second-rate world of selfish people who keep screwing up, over and over. Only love motivates the Son to give Himself up, to be cut off from the lifeblood of His Father's love, to die on a cross so that we can share in that same love. This same Love leaves behind His Spirit descending like a dove into the living room of our hearts.

If we do not serve and minister out of the Father's love, our works are futile and often self-serving. Without love we create a merit system and emphasize works instead of relationship. The prophet Jeremiah describes what happens when we do this: "My people have . . . forsaken me, the spring of living water, and have dug their own cisterns, broken cisterns that cannot hold water" (Jeremiah 2:13). The Israelites consistently created idols and followed their own selfish whims. Jesus fired a similar charge at the Pharisees, who became so consumed with doing that they forgot why they were supposedly serving in the first place: "Woe to you, teachers of the law and Pharisees, you hypocrites! You clean the outside of the cup and dish, but inside they are full of greed and self-indulgence" (Matthew 23:25). Like the church at Ephesus, the Pharisees had lost their first love (Revelation 2:4).

Paul defines love from the same standard that Jesus established. From his famous description of love in 1 Corinthians 13, we're reminded that we cannot love selflessly on our own, only as a reflection of the Father's love for us.

Love never gives up.
Love cares more for others than for self.

Love doesn't want what it doesn't have.
Love doesn't strut,
Doesn't have a swelled head,
Doesn't force itself on others,
Isn't always "me first,"
Doesn't fly off the handle,
Doesn't keep score of the sins of others,
Doesn't revel when others grovel,
Takes pleasure in the flowering of truth,
Puts up with anything,
Trusts God always,
Always looks for the best,
Never looks back,
But keeps going to the end.
Love never dies. (13:4-8, MSG)

As we sort through all kinds of worthwhile demands on our time and energy, how do we apply Paul's definition of love to our lives? How do we serve in a way that always trusts God and never gives up? In order to identify the service God has called and gifted us to do, it helps to recall how Paul applied Christ's love in his own life ministry. A closer look at the man who penned 1 Corinthians 13 offers insight about how our love for God can help clarify how we serve Him.

Paul spoke and acted from the depths of his desire for Christ. He endured a catalog of trials and tortures that would put most of us to shame:

Five times I received from the Jews thirty-nine lashes. Three times I was beaten with rods, once I was stoned, three times I was shipwrecked, a night and a day I have spent in the deep. I have been on frequent journeys, in dangers from rivers, dangers from robbers, dangers from my countrymen, dangers from the Gentiles, dangers in the city, dangers in the wilderness, dangers on the sea, dangers among false brethren; I have been in labor and hardship, through many sleepless nights, in hunger and thirst, often without food, in cold and exposure. Apart from such external things, there is the daily pressure upon me of concern for all the churches. (2 Corinthians 11:24-28, NASB)

Paul's life was a cross between the lifestyles of Indiana Jones, Billy Graham, and the president. What in the world would sustain someone to endure such difficulties without giving up or killing himself? It makes me reconsider my grumbling complaints about burnout, teaching overload, lack of time, and unappreciative people.

Paul's secret? A blinding love that literally stopped him cold in his tracks. Before he met Christ, he was a bounty hunter of Christians, continually in hot pursuit of those he despised for their faith and their resistance to Jewish law. One evening, just on the outskirts of the city of Damascus, "he was suddenly dazed by a blinding flash of light. As he fell to the ground, he head a voice: 'Saul, Saul, why are you out to get me?'" (Acts 9:3-4, MSG). Saul of Tarsus become Paul, Apostle to the Gentiles, a man whose supernatural contribution to God's kingdom is immeasurable.

Frederick Buechner, in his book *The Longing for Home* wrote: "God . . . loved [Paul] enough to save him — him of all people — and from that day forward every word he ever wrote and every weary mile he ever traveled sprang from his passion to touch the heart of the world as his own heart had been touched by the revelation of that extraordinary moment."[5]

May I Or Must I?

When we realize, as Paul did, the extent of God's love for us, it is life-changing, for it stops us in our tracks and wraps us in a blinding illumination of our Father's love. Our moments of service have their roots in the seeds of love showered mercifully like rain upon the hardest, most stubborn soil of our hearts. This is the kind of love required to cultivate any and every ministry.

When we forget, ignore, or fail to explore the reality of God's love, our acts and ministries become unbearable burdens. As Hannah Whitall Smith explains in her classic *The Christian's Secret of a Happy Life*, "The soul finds itself saying, instead of the 'May I?' of love, the 'Must I?' of duty. The yoke, which was at first easy, begins to gall, and the burden feels heavy instead of light."[6] A prayer-centered life is a life lived in the bull's-eye of God's love for you. Otherwise, you miss the target and shoot aimless arrows out of your own efforts.

When we feel close to burning out in our ministries, when we are serving yet spiritually starving, we grit our teeth and try harder. To give up would be defeat. It would give others the impression that we're not spiritually mature enough to handle the job. We must shatter this self-concerned, self-conscious view of service and realize that burnout or spiritual famine should point us back to our source, our relationship with God. Burnout and spiritual hunger signal our need for a getaway with our Lover. We need silence, a spiritual vacation alone with our Father, like Christ's retreats to the lonely places and mountainsides.

If we do not heed burnout as a signal for prayer and retreat, we end up lost in our own efforts, burning without light. I learned this the hard way. When I first started teaching college English almost ten years ago, I had more to learn than my students. I had endured the usual graduate class on teaching techniques and I had tutored as a teaching assistant for other professors. But on my own I soon discovered that I was much more concerned with everything else but what I supposedly cared most about, instructing other people about writing. I worried about whether they would like me, so I worked to be hip and funny and one of them. I worried almost as much about whether they would respect me, so I gave pop quizzes and took attendance every day and wore professorial-looking ties. I worried about discipline and grading and whether I was teaching them anything at all. I worried about all the externals.

Since those first few semesters, I've learned to teach because I love to teach. Sure, I still worry about what my students think of me, and about the techniques, content, and methodology I use. But I've learned to relax and put my heart into why I wanted to teach in the first place. I love to write, and I love passing that passion on to some unassuming person who thinks writing is simply putting commas in mysteriously arbitrary places. Because I care deeply about language and how it works and what we say and how we say it, I've found that the other elements take care of themselves with adequate preparation. In fact, the preparation becomes enjoyable because I know I get to discuss something I love with a semi-captive audience. The externals that I used to worry about so much become natural extensions of what I care about.

I returned to love as my motivator for teaching because that's what I discovered in my other "official" ministries. I used to feel pressure from counselors, church teachers, or pastors to go on visitation, attend prayer vigils, or help in the soup kitchen. I believed I had to serve God in these ways in order to prove I loved Him. I later realized I was trying to prove it to others instead of to God. At the time, I didn't take much time to reflect on it. I just visited, prayed, and ladled soup dutifully.

Finally, I began to notice that something was terribly wrong with me. The things I enjoyed doing—writing, reading, teaching, even praying—were luxuries for which I never had time, while the things I was doing to prove my faith seemed unbearable. I wondered if my faith had really set, or if others felt this way too. As I began to talk to others and read Scripture, I became convinced that I had it backwards. My service must come out of my love for God, not a reluctant, guilt-induced slavery that ground me down to a fine powder.

Months of prayer confirmed that my old distorted view had to change. I quit doing all the service activities I'd signed up for. I slowly, gradually began committing only to serve in areas in which I felt God's leading, and His gifting. Prayer—sustained conversation with my Father—would determine how I acted on my love for Him. I realize how dangerous this could have been, how I could have used this to exploit God's gracious freedom. Thankfully, that first time, I did not. My honest dialogue with God clarified and focused what He would have me do.

The Ladder of Prayer

What I discovered through prayer was a magnificent freedom, the freedom that comes from belonging to someone. When tempted to prove my spirituality to others or to please them, I talked to God and was reminded of who I am as His child.

What I experienced applies to us all. Not only are we free from the guilt, pressure, and frustration of forcing ourselves to do things we're not called to, but there's also a freedom from the blame we often shift to God when we're not serving the "right way." His love frees us and requires only that we love others with the same freedom, the same selflessness.

Once we have discovered the joyous security of His love for us, all the old try-harder efforts seem second-rate by comparison. Instead there's a longing to give ourselves, to do everything He asks us to do. Eugene Peterson expresses it well: "The Christian is the person who recognizes that our real problem is not in achieving freedom but in learning service under a better master. The Christian recognizes that every relationship that excludes God becomes oppressive. Recognizing and realizing that, we urgently want to live under the mastery of God."[7] That's not to say I still don't wake up in the middle of a church business committee and wonder why I'm there. But at least now I'm quicker to return to my Father's lap to explore my contribution to such service.

This kind of freedom, based on our acceptance and awareness of His love and grace, must be the beginning point for service. If prayer must be a loving communiqué with our Abba Father, then service must be a loving product of our relationship.

> My dear, dear friends, if God loved us like this, we
> certainly ought to love each other. No one has seen God,
> ever. But if we love one another, God dwells deeply within
> us, and his love becomes complete in us — perfect love! . . .
> When we take up permanent residence in a life of love, we
> live in God and God lives in us.
> (1 John 4:11-12,16, MSG)

Francis de Sales, a French Jesuit who eventually became bishop of Geneva in 1602, describes the relationship between prayer and service in his "Introduction to the Devout Life." In the midst of a Catholic system that relied heavily on deeds and penance, Francis urged believers to see their "one true devotion," which he defines as "simply true love of God." He viewed this as the foundation for any attempt at ministry:

> Since devotion consists in a certain degree of eminent char-
> ity, it not only makes us prompt, active, and faithful in
> observance of God's commands, but in addition it arouses

us to do quickly and lovingly as many good works as possible, both those commanded and those merely counseled
or inspired.

This "eminent charity" he defines as "spiritual fire," the passion that fuels
our expression of loving service, "devotion." He extends his explanation by comparing the relationship between prayer and service to Jacob's
ladder: "The two sides between which we climb upward and to which
the rungs are fastened represent *prayer,* which calls down *God's love,* and
sacraments, which confer it" (emphasis added).[8] In other words, the ladder of prayer we climb brings down God's love which fuels our actions
back on the ground.

We are called to live our prayers, prompted by love and dependence upon the Father. Christian service is not the drudgery of slavery.
Ministry is the way we live in a love relationship with our Father, the
way we act that shows His love to others. Slavery resentfully endures a
nameless, feckless master; the other feels privileged to serve a lover.

Francis de Sales's view of the marriage between prayer and service
as the expression of God's love reminds me of my courtship with my
wife. As we stood comfortably quiet under a quilt of stars next to the
inky dark waters of Lake Loudon, I recognized the seed of love for her
in my heart. Consequently, I continued to see her, to write poems for
her; I gave her a silver locket, called her, got to know her. My love deep-
ened and I wanted to express it by asking her to marry me on bended
knee with a ring in hand. My action would have been meaningless if
not for the passion that infused it. It was the same with our wedding
ceremony. The exchange of rings and vows would mean nothing if we
did not love each other. That is as it should be, in marriage, and in
divine marriage, the union of our heart and soul to the One who loves
us most. "Living in awareness of our belovedness is the axis around
which the Christian life revolves."[9]

How do we live out our prayers? How do we know which committee to serve on, which cause to volunteer for, which Sunday school
class to teach, which potluck to orchestrate? Which job should we pursue, which missions trip embark upon? Which people at work should
we discuss our most intimate relationship with? The answers vary for

each of us. We love first and serve as God reveals His will to us. The action comes from inside our hearts, from prompting by the Holy Spirit, from the only true source of love, not the other way around. All service and ministry must start from love, otherwise we end up doing it for ourselves.

No one can tell you what service you are called to. Others can recommend good works and areas of service, such as giving your time and money, caring for orphans and widows, the needy, the hungry and homeless, the imprisoned. But the litmus test of what service is right for you is your love for the Father. Examine your heart. Talk to your Abba Father. He will bring forth fruit that will blossom and flourish for a hungry world of people.

Questions for Prayer and Reflection

1. What is your response to the kind of love poems and prayers written by previous Christians such as the mystics? Do you feel embarrassed, moved, surprised, detached, sad, disappointed, joyful when you read them? Read the Song of Songs and consider what it means to view your love relationship with God in comparison to a romance.

2. Make a list of all the service activities penciled in on your calendar. What is your response to each one? (If you don't have a response, that should tell you something, too.) How many of these activities fit into "things I want to do" versus "things I have to do"? Jot down your feelings for each activity or ministry. Prayerfully lift each one up and seek the Father's will as to how you can best express your love for Him.

3. Think back to times in your life when you've genuinely experienced the joy of serving God. Journal on what you were doing; focus on why you enjoyed giving yourself in this way. How do those times compare with your present service?

4. Think about jobs you've done for God in which you felt inadequate or unqualified. How did God work through you despite your reservations and/or weaknesses?

5. What role does freedom play in the acts of ministry and service we live out? How are you experiencing this freedom presently?

O God, you are the light of the minds that know you,
the life of the souls that love you, and the strength
of the wills that serve you; help us so to know you that
we may truly love you, so to love you that we may
fully serve you, whom to serve is perfect freedom;
through Jesus Christ our Lord.[10]

—ST. AUGUSTINE OF HIPPO

HEARING GOD'S VOICE

"Listen! My beloved! Behold, he is coming,
climbing on the mountains, leaping on the hills! I was asleep,
but my heart was awake. A voice!
My beloved was knocking."

—SONG OF SONGS 2:8, 5:2 (NASB)

"My sheep hear My voice,
and I know them, and they follow Me."

—JOHN 10:27 (NASB)

One friend experiences God's voice while driving down the highway, complete with the physical sensation of being hugged. Another goes on regular retreats for the sole purpose of listening to God. Many of the mystics heard the Father speak in monasteries, convents, and on mountaintops.

I hear Him in my own life, but describing His voice or examining how He speaks is as elusive and overwhelming as collecting the ocean in my hand. If we are tempted to formulize, package, and control prayer as a skill or activity to be checked off our spiritual to-do list, then we'll also be tempted to underestimate or ignore the importance of hearing God's voice.

Before we go any further, let's define what we mean by "God's voice." It would be so much easier if we could hear God's voice the way my children hear my voice calling them across the playground. Then we could ask others if they heard it, too, and what they make of it.

Hearing God Inside and Out

For various reasons, God no longer speaks in an audible voice. Instead, through the gift of the Holy Spirit, we experience God's indwelling presence. His Spirit leads and guides us and "intercedes for us with groans that words cannot express" (Romans 8:26). The act of depending on the Holy Spirit to discern God's voice for us also forces us to rely more on faith than the "factual" proof we so often crave. The Spirit also allows God to customize our relationship with Him, in a sense, to nourish and cultivate and relate with the unique man or woman each of us is. He does this by making us sensitive to God's timing in our lives, by making us aware of His presence in others and in His creation, and by utilizing our unique abilities and resources. God uses His Spirit as His voice within us to prompt our hearts to love, serve, and obey Him.

God also speaks to us from external sources, often through the words of others and through the medium of our own thoughts. As we see throughout the Scriptures, especially with the Old Testament prophets, God often used other people to speak His message, whether prophetic, instructional, or exhortative. Hosea prophesied to the northern kingdom (Israel) that their nation would be exiled for rebellion against God and then be restored because of God's love for them. At the same time, the prophet Isaiah delivered a similar message to Judah. Or consider Jonah, who anticipated such a positive reception of God's message from the people of Nineveh that he tried to run away, only to be swallowed by a great fish. These prophets often forecasted God's plan of salvation through the coming of Christ. They delivered language based on the message God laid on their hearts, and the people heard God speak through their voices.

God also chose to inspire human scribes to record His message in the form of the Bible. This does not mean He uses people as mere conduits of communication, as we would pick up a cellular phone. Instead, "God and the person 'used' speak conjointly. And it may be that the one spoken to is also the one spoken through. The word is at once the Word of God, God speaking, and the word of a human being who also is speaking."[1]

Other than through spoken language, many critics and scholars believe that God reveals Himself and His message for us primarily through three points or "lights": life circumstances, personal impressions from the Holy Spirit, and His Word. In his classic book *The Secret of Guidance*, F. B. Meyer wrote:

> God's impressions within and his word without are always corroborated by his providence around, and we should quietly wait until those three focus into one point. . . . If you do not know what you ought to do, stand still until you do. And when the time comes for action, circumstances, like glowworms, will sparkle along your path; and you will become so sure that you are right, when God's three witnesses concur, that you could not be surer though an angel beckoned you on.[2]

Clack-clack of God's Voice

Meyer's view correlates to what many contemporary scholars and writers share about the way God speaks in their lives. Writer Frederick Buechner asserts, "At its heart most theology, like most fiction, is essentially autobiography."[3] He reckons, "If there is a God who speaks anywhere, surely he speaks here: through waking up and working, through going away and coming back again, through people you meet and books you read, through falling asleep in the dark."[4] If we listen intently, Buechner instructs, God speaks intently, deliberately, through all the nuances of our day. His voice may be subtle as a whisper, as loud as thunder, unexpectedly tender, or remarkably firm. Rarely in this life is it all we desire, but rather what we need in the moment: music to dance to, a child's cry for comfort, a lover's whisper, an angry retort.

Buechner lives out what he teaches. In his novel, *The Final Beast,* a young pastor named Nicolet, widowed with two small girls, begins to examine his faith. Lying in a grassy field near his father's home in the New England countryside, Nicolet becomes Everyone as he listens for God:

> "Please," he whispered. Still flat on his back, he stretched out his fists as far as they would reach— "Please . . ."—then opened them, palms up, and held them there as he watched for something, for the air to cleave, fold back like a tent flap, to let a

splendor through. The air would part like a curtain, and the
splendor would not break or bend anything but only fill the
empty places between the trees, the trees and the house, between
his hands, which he brought together now. Nothing was happening except that everything that he could see—the shabby barn,
weeds, orchard—had too much the look of nothing happening.

Two apple branches struck against each other with the lim-
ber clack of wood on wood. That was all—a tick-tock rattle of
branches—but then a fierce lurch of excitement at what was
only daybreak, only the smell of summer coming, only starting
back again for home, but oh Jesus, he thought, with a great
lump in his throat and a crazy grin, it was an agony of gladness
and beauty falling wild and soft like rain. Just clack-clack, but
praise him, he thought. Praise him. Maybe all his journeying,
he thought, had been only to bring him here to hear two
branches hit each other twice like that, to see nothing cross the
threshold but to see the threshold, to hear the dry clack-clack
of the world's tongue at the approach of the approach perhaps
of splendor.[5]

How do you respond to the clack-clack of apple branches God
telegraphs your way? How often do any of us stop to listen, to ask, to
seek what God sends, not what we imagine He should send? For most
of us, it takes something a bit more overt, a convergence of points.
Sometimes we have to be hit over the head with the very present God
speaks to us.

Resistance to His Direction
It is often this way with me. When I was falling in love with my wife,
everything I encountered, each of the three lights, directed my heart to
the prospect of marrying her. I'd never experienced this with the other
women I'd dated. I first recognized the convergence while Dotti was
away for a beach vacation with several of her girlfriends. First, circumstances consistently reminded me of her and my longing for her every-
where I turned. I was caught off guard. Up until this time, we were
simply friends who enjoyed each other's company. Our few months

together was one of the few times I had enjoyed the company of the oppo-site sex without feeling pressured to see what would happen romantically.

Naturally, I was a bit testy when my pastor, with whom I was counseling at the time, happened to ask, "So, things are really going well with Dotti?"

"Well, yeah," I answered, reluctant to acknowledge much more than a friendship with her. "No big deal, though. We're just enjoying becoming friends."

"That's good," he said, knowingly. "I think God's up to something there."

I smiled and changed the subject, resenting his attempt at divine matchmaking, which I'd experienced unsuccessfully with other well-intended believers before. However, I couldn't shake his words.

In my Bible readings, I read passages like 1 John 4 and 1 Corin-thians 13. There was something nagging inside me about my feelings for Dotti; they were different—a different shape, deeper, more intri-cate—from any I'd ever had before for another person. The best I can put words to it, there was something transcendent, something totally selfish and yet selfless about the way I was feeling for her.

Nonetheless, I had my grab bag of excuses handy. I wasn't ready to commit. I was too young, according to my timetable. I was still in grad school. I didn't have a job. My personal life and addictive struggles were not yet resolved (as if they ever truly are).

Yet my feelings persisted. The separation was much more painful and lonely than I could have anticipated. It wasn't just the usual I'm-dating-someone-and-now-I'm-alone-and-miss-her kind of thing. I missed *her.* I found myself in the library, supposedly writing a paper on the poetry of Robert Browning, taking my class ring off my right hand and placing it backwards on my left hand like a wedding band. It terrified me. What was I doing?

I ended up setting a fleece (recall Gideon's example in Judges 6:36-40), something I do not recommend any more than proof texting—randomly opening the Bible and forcing a passage to apply to your life. It's much more likely that we misuse such tests as gimmicks to get what we want. Nevertheless, at that time I prayed and decided that if Dotti brought me back a gift (we were not at a stage where it was assumed she would even think of me, let alone bring back a gift), then that would validate my feelings and conviction to pursue marrying her. Since she was the other half of this divine telegram, I decided that if she brought a gift, then she was at least thinking of me while she was away.

She called shortly after she returned and invited me to dinner. Over quiche and Waldorf salad, as she related her time at the beach, she finally handed me a tiny box, saying, "I thought you might like this." I froze.

Every bell and whistle went off inside me. Here it was—the dew was on the fleece, just as I had asked. I unwrapped the box and found a miniature duck decoy, something Dotti knew I collected. Holy, sacred, silly little duck.

Things moved rapidly from there. A couple of days later I spilled my guts to her, partially because I wanted her to know exactly how I was feeling and what was going on, and partially because I wanted it to end right there if she wasn't receptive to our relationship deepening. But she was. And six months later we walked down the aisle.

It was one of only a few times in my life when I knew without a doubt what God wanted me to do, when I felt His pleasure and reassurance at every step. A few other men had told me, "You'll know when the right woman comes along," and I'd always doubted and resented the subjectivity of such a marker. And I still feel that way. Even having participated in it and experienced it, I still hate to tell my single friends, "You'll know." There's so much more to it than that. And yet, as F. B. Meyer points out, when God speaks in our lives, there is indeed a convergence of events and feelings and Scripture that's like a neon sign pointing the way.

Choosing to Listen

I want to add one more thing to this story. At the time it was clear in my mind that I still had a choice. I didn't have to act on my feelings and awareness of God's voice concerning this woman. I could run and hide. I could let all my fears and doubts drown out my Father's clear tone. But I also knew that if I ran I would end up in a fish's belly, regretting an incredible gift that He had given me.

We often allow our fears to fuel our excuses. Then we remove ourselves from the responsibility and risk of responding and acting.

It's what we see with Moses in his mixed response to conversing with God in the burning bush:

> Now Moses was tending the flock of Jethro his father-in-law, the priest of Midian, and he led the flock to the far side of the desert and came to Horeb, the mountain of God. There the angel of the LORD appeared to him in flames of fire from within a bush. Moses saw that though the bush was on fire it did not burn up. So Moses thought, "I will go over and see this strange sight—why the bush does not burn up."
>
> When the LORD saw that he had gone over to look, God called to him from within the bush, "Moses! Moses!"
>
> And Moses said, "Here I am."
>
> "Do not come any closer," God said. "Take off your sandals, for the place where you are standing is holy ground." (Exodus 3:1-5)

As God reveals His message to Moses, the shepherd begins to make excuse after excuse for not leading God's people—what if they ask who sent me . . . what if they don't believe me? I'm just not eloquent enough, Lord.

Patiently, God persists and has answers for each of Moses' contingencies. After all of Moses' excuses are answered, the decision is still up to Moses. As we saw in the last chapter, our response to God's love is still up to us. As compelling as our Father's voice of love is, we are still autonomous beings who choose how to respond. Even when all three lights burn brightly toward one direction, we can still rebel. Often we do this under a spiritual guise.

We must be very careful not to contrive a convergence to suit our will when we seek His voice. It can be easy to convince oneself of a convergence by using circular reasoning to interpret the other points: "I feel that God is leading me to the mission field; and since I don't like my job right now, maybe that's the circumstance I've been waiting on." Or what about that person with whom you've gone on a couple of dates who proposes marriage prematurely by insisting, "God has spoken to me and told me we're perfect for each other" while you feel and hear nothing and wonder if the person has just escaped from the latest cult.

Clearly, we have to be wary of trusting ourselves too much. We have to listen with our hearts attuned to God's voice rather than our own desires. Jesus instructs, "He who has ears, let him hear" (Matthew 11:15). Since listening will continue to be a subjective process, the process gets difficult at times, even for the most well-intended, mature believer.

Yet I also believe that if we honestly pursue God's message for us, we will know the difference between His voice and the wild rambling of our own thoughts. As Dallas Willard points out, "The voice of God is not itself any one of the three lights, nor all of them together. But the inner teaching of which John speaks in his first epistle—the voice or Word of God coming to individuals, as repeatedly displayed in biblical events—*usually* comes to us in conjunction with responsible study and meditation on the Bible, with experience of the various kinds of movements of the Spirit in our hearts, and with intelligent alertness to circumstances that befall us."[6]

This kind of message from God tends to be directional, providing guidance and pointing the way along the decision-strewn path we're on. While God often speaks to us this way, He also gives us messages that affirm, chastise, protect, reassure, or simply reveal His character to us. Out of a season of physical exhaustion and spiritual dryness, Brennan Manning describes a spiritual retreat in which he waited and waited on God to speak to him. The message he finally received was so simple as to be unexpected: "Live in the wisdom of accepted tenderness."[7]

After receiving a wedding proposal from a godly man she loved, one of our dear friends still felt terribly afraid and uncertain. But then she heard God say tenderly, "Fear not."

Every Breath I Take

For myself, I think of a pop song that God has set up as a recurring theme in my life, a reminder of His loving presence. Shortly after I became a Christian, I struggled with addiction and depression. As I sat in the university cafeteria with a new, more spiritually mature friend, I confessed that so much of my relationship with God revolved around feeling unloved, around my distrust of God. Arrogant and insecure, I couldn't believe that He would love me. My friend kept speaking to my deaf ears verses of Scripture about my Abba's love.

As we sat there in silence, I had him stumped. Music droned in the background over the auditorium-style speakers. The clatter of silverware punctuated dozens of conversations across the dining hall.

"Listen," Tad said. "Do you hear that?"

"What?"

"That song. Do you know it?"

We strained to hear the music above the other conversations and kitchen noises. "Yeah, I know it," I said. "It's the Police—'Every Breath You Take.'"

"What's it about?" Tad asked, persistently. "Have you listened to the words before?"

"Basically, it sounds like it's a lover stalking someone who dumped him."

We both laughed.

"Yeah, well, God's like that, too," Tad said. "He stalks us with His love. He knows how many hairs are on your head and how many breaths you take. He loves you—*you*—like that. I hope every time you hear that song it reminds you of His breath on your face."

I shrugged, yet inwardly I was taken aback at the thought of God caring about me that intimately. Needless to say, the song has buoyed to the surface of my life at surprisingly unexpected moments—as I flip on the radio, in the background of a restaurant, at a friend's house—during times when I desperately needed to be reminded of His love. I know, it's just coincidence—divine coincidence.

The Voice of Silence

You probably have your own songs, poems, and words that broadcast the Father's love to you. You've likely experienced God's other mode of communication to us as well. He doesn't use only His voice when He communicates with us. He uses silence as well. In fact, there are at least two aspects of His silence. One is the comfortable silence of simply being still in His presence and knowing that He is God and that He loves us. The second is the almost unbearably painful silence when we long for Him to speak. This silence we often perceive as His absence, which also points us back to His presence by negation. It points us back to our longing, our desire, our hope in Him that is enforced by remembering what His voice sounds like.

We usually welcome and seek out the first kind of silence. Often we delight in doing nothing other than resting before God, reminded of His love, of His presence, of His mercy to us. After a long absence from someone we love, words often get in the way. The real communication takes place in silence, in the embrace or in the locking of eyes.

I think again of how things began with Dotti. We were friends and had talked pleasantly throughout dinner. Afterward, we drove through the curving snake of back roads out to the lake. And there the evening converged in a stillness, a calm that mirrored the placid summer water. Stars kited above us like distant birds with diamond beaks, the moon a giant pearl. A lonesome boat trolled its red-green light across the dark horizon. We stood there, next to each other on the bank, just stood there. The silence was frightening in its intimacy. I was so comfortable with her quiet that there was no need to pursue chitchat, no need to worry about what she was thinking. I thought later, as we drove away, that I could marry this woman then and there. Her warm, communicative silence was so inviting.

God's silence is even more luxurious and inviting. We bask in the quiet He affords our souls amidst life's cacophony of urgent voices and noisy distractions. He is quiet. He is tender. He speaks wordlessly, lovingly.

While we welcome this kind of silence, too often we seek it without its twin, the silence of God that feels like absence. It's easy to romanticize the former if we attempt to describe it without considering the ache we experience when it seems like He's not there. This silence can be incredibly frustrating, irritating, and annoying. It feels like He's silent because He doesn't care. On the other hand, we're supposed to believe by faith that He's there always, never abandoning us, as He has promised (Matthew 28:20; Hebrews 13:5). Many times in my life God has remained silent when I begged and pleaded for any word or sign from Him. I usually retaliated by withdrawing, pouting into my own silence of absence.

When we focus on ourselves, the act of listening and waiting for

God's voice becomes a rather tiresome, endless, futile endeavor, much like Vladimir and Estragon experience in Samuel Beckett's *Waiting for Godot*. They wait and chatter ceaselessly about the impending arrival of the inscrutable Godot, who never arrives. They discuss all the activities they will complete once Godot arrives. They make note of all the questions they need Godot to answer before they can continue on their journey. They make their entire lives conditional on Godot appearing at their particular spot in the road.

While we are called to wait on God, we must not use this to become passive, self-protectors. When the focus is on ourselves, and God's voice is perceived as a condition of our personal happiness, then we are likely never to hear Him satisfactorily. Too often, under the guise of being spiritual, we try to force God into an Aladdin's lamp in which we control when we'll beckon Him. He doesn't relate with us in that way.

I'm not saying we shouldn't feel many of the emotions that arise when we can't feel our Father's presence. In fact, we should feel them — they testify to our longing for Him. But we must keep our faith alive at these times, trusting that He will reveal Himself again in good time. Faith is not fueled by our feelings but by the hope we cling to in Christ.

In Chaim Potok's powerful novel, *The Chosen*, the narrator's friend, Danny, experiences a similar silence from his earthly father. Raised in the strict Hassidic culture of Judaism, Danny is a sensitive son expected to follow in the footsteps of his tzaddik father. Due to the father's lack of involvement with him, however, there's nothing desirable or meaningful in this pursuit. What Danny longs for most—his father's approval, affirmation, and embrace—are withheld from him. He rages and only finds relief in his academic pursuits. Finally, as an adult, Danny learns that his father's silence was a loving gift. His father loved his son so much that he sincerely believed the son would grow and develop as God intended him to, as a religious leader, if he sacrificially detached himself from his son. The silence was a kind of training or preparation.

Perhaps this is the same kind of loving absence we see Jesus experience on the cross in His most desperate hour: "*Eli, Eli, lama sabachthani?*" ("My God, my God, why have you forsaken me?", Matthew 27:46).

Love requires separation at times, a sacrifice for a higher unseen purpose, a reminder of what and who we long for. The old adage "Distance makes the heart grow fonder or makes it wander" seems so apt for us as Christians. Typically, when we experience this kind of absence we feel hurt, angry, sad. We wander away from waiting on Him and we drift into the mirage of greener, idolatrous pastures because they afford immediate relief.

Entering the Silence

How can we seek God even when He feels absent? What would it be like to welcome, even seek out, this kind of experience? I believe the answer is to embrace the suffering. I believe suffering often stretches us beyond what we think we are capable. Such experiences are as hellish and tormenting as being lost in the Mojave. That's why it seems easier to complain and rage than to accept whatever message lies in the silence.

We see this expressed in innumerable ways by our society, by both Christians and nonbelievers, when God doesn't come through the way we expect or want. This is the kind of attitude expressed in Tony Kushner's provocative epic play, *Angels in America,* which says that God has basically run away from home and abandoned His creation as a failed experiment.

On the rare occasions when I've accepted God's silence rather than raged against it or withdrawn in retaliation, I've experienced a deepening of soul, a renewal of faith, and an overjoyed refreshment when God "reappeared." Such times are not comfortable or conducive to our schedules, but they can purge and purify our desires in ways that hearing God cannot.

Like Job's excruciating experience of God's absence, we must ask ourselves not only, "Where are You?" but "Will I keep waiting and looking for You?" If we stop with the first question we are alleviated of responsibility; we are justified to fulfill ourselves or worship idols, because God didn't do His part. Yet if we push through the first question to the second, then we are forced to be just as responsible as God. This leads us to ask what it is about God we're really after. Are we after what He does for us, or who He is? Once again, we're forced to choose between the urgency of self and the eternity of relationship.

Every time one of my close friends moves across the country, I am forced to confront my emotions. Will I detach myself from this person so that I will not hurt with his departure, or will I allow my heart to ache with the cavity of his absence? Will I continue to love him, which in this case means I will suffer our apartness?

Likewise with God, we are allowed to honestly express ourselves; but ultimately we choose how we respond to His silence. If we dare trust God despite these moments, we gain a wider perspective of His goodness and His character, in which both are necessary and consequential. As C. S. Lewis so aptly put it, "Pain is God's megaphone to a deaf world." Ironically, the pain of silence can restore our hearing if we are willing to listen.

In her poem "Behold a Shaking," poet Christina Rosetti captures this perspective:

Blessed that flock safe penned in Paradise;
Blessed this flock which tramps in weary ways;
All form one flock, God's flock; all yield Him praise
By joy, or pain, still tending toward the prize.
Joy speaks in praises there, and sings and flies
Where no night is, exulting all its days;
Here, pain finds solace, for, behold, it prays;
In *both* love lives the life that never dies.[8]
(emphasis added)

It is only when we can allow our pain to fuel our heart's true longing that we grow closer to God.

God speaks to us in a myriad ways: through the Spirit-led voice of our thoughts and emotions, through the human voices of others, through Scripture, through circumstances, through silence. Yes, even through a song on the radio. Hearing God's voice, filtering it above the clamor of our lives, is not easy. It requires a prayer-centered communicator who is willing to pause, to listen, to reflect, to act. It requires that we remember that prayer is a *two*-way communication. Above all, it requires a hunger for holiness that will only continue to grow until we are famished for Him in this life, and only satiated in the next.

Questions for Prayer and Reflection

1. How have you experienced God's voice in the past? What did you feel during those times? What actions did you pursue as a result of what you experienced and felt?

2. What is the hardest part of discerning God's voice for you? Have there been times when you've been deceived by your own selfish desires? How can you tell the difference between His voice and other voices, including your own, that seek to direct you?

3. Can you recall a time when God spoke to you through something as subtle or mundane as apple branches clacking together or a song on the radio? How do you respond to Buechner's assertion that God speaks to us every day through its events, along with our memories and emotions?

4. What's your typical response when a once-dear friend no longer returns your calls or letters? What keeps you from responding the same way when God is silent?

5. What is God saying to you right now—through the events of today, through that nagging verse of Scripture that keeps coming to mind, through this book, through the person you care about most? How will you respond?

—

Talk with us, Lord, thyself reveal
While here o'er earth we rove;
Speak to our hearts, and let us feel
The kindling of thy love.

With thee conversing we forget
All time, and toil, and care:
Labour is rest, and pain is sweet
If thou, my God art here.

Here then, my God, vouchsafe to stay,
And bid my heart rejoice;
My bounding heart shall own thy sway,
And echo to thy voice.

Thou callest me to seek thy face—
'Tis all I wish to seek;
To attend the whispers of thy grace,
And hear thee inly speak.

Let this my every hour employ,
Till I thy glory see,
Enter into my Master's joy,
And find my heaven in thee.[9]

—CHARLES WESLEY

RESTLESS PEACE

Now we see but a poor reflection as in a mirror,
then we shall see face to face.
Now I know in part; then I shall know fully,
even as I am fully known.

—1 CORINTHIANS 13:12

Author Anne Lamott recounts the story of her friend who took her two-year-old with her on vacation. The friend obtained a suite with two rooms, one to work in and the other to sleep in. Late one afternoon, she heard her son knocking on the closed door that connected their rooms. He had managed to lock the door. His room was in complete darkness and now he couldn't get to the person who loved him most.

His mother tried to talk him through unlocking the door. He couldn't do it. She then called the manager, the fire department, and anybody else who might know what to do. It was going to take a while. In the meantime, her little boy sobbed in the dark, terrified and confused. "Finally," Anne says, "she did the only thing she could, which was to slide her fingers underneath the door, where there was a one-inch space. She kept telling him over and over to bend down and find her fingers. Finally somehow he did."

The mother wanted to make more calls, to do something, but she felt like contact with her son was the most important thing. So she kept holding onto him with her fingers under the door, talking to him, telling him little stories. Finally she got him to try jiggling the lock again and it opened.

"I kept thinking of that story, how much it feels like I'm the two-year-old in the dark and God is the mother, and I don't speak the language. She could break down the door if that struck her as being the best way, and ride off with me on her charger. But instead, via my friends and my church and my shabby faith, I can just hold onto her fingers underneath the door. It isn't enough, and it is." [1]

Lamott's story reminds me of a recent conversation I had. My friend and I were lamenting the trials of a couple from church whose newborn needed a heart transplant. "The longer I live, the more I long for heaven," my friend said earnestly.

"It's hard to understand why things like this happen," I said.

"Yes, and to keep loving and trusting God even as we wonder." My friend's tone of voice turned wistful. "The older I get, the more I'm forced to rely on prayer, to trust God. I realize how little control I have over life. It seems ironic that the older I get, there are also more people in my life to love, and I hope, more of God's love in my own life."

"I don't like hearing you say that," I confessed. "I'd rather believe that the older I get, the more control I have over life. Instead of age bringing wisdom—which seems to be greater trust in God—I want management."

"Don't count on it," she said, and chuckled. "Besides, that's not what you really want. You want heaven."

Lamott's story and my recent conversation echo the same theme. We are called to struggle without giving up, to hurt without abandoning God, to rejoice for what He gives. This is perhaps the most satisfying and most troubling fruit of prayer. I call this paradoxical fruit of the prayer-centered life 'restless peace'.

Aches of Contentment

Restless peace is the contentment that comes from living life with a purpose beyond the next job, the upcoming vacation, or a more loving partner. This peace is also the terrible ache of acutely loving Christ and pursuing Him with all your heart, mind, and soul. And knowing your desire for Him only gets worse before it gets better.

Restless peace produces a wild gratitude for both the dark nights of the soul and the gold-fringed dawns of rising again with Him. Living a prayer-centered life amounts to living with a crazy supernatural love always bubbling at the crust of your soul. The peace comes as a gift, as the product of knowing and trusting your Father more each day. We are created for deep, abiding relationship with Him and the better we know and love Him, the more contentment we feel in our souls. Such relational intimacy will not be consummated in this lifetime. It requires patience. In fact, as my wife tells our daughter, we have to *practice* patience. But we taste moments of His presence, hear the sweetness of His voice, taste the depth of His love in ways that leave us aching for all of Him. We grow more restless in this life even as we grow in contented joy at knowing God.

Not as the World Gives

Jesus told His disciples, "Peace I leave with you; My peace I give to you; not as the world gives, do I give to you. Let not your heart be troubled, nor let it be fearful" (John 14:27, NASB). The catch, of course, is the "not as the world gives" part. God's peace is much richer and more abiding. It's hard to put our finger on because we don't know anything like it. In fact, to make sure we ponder His supernatural definition, on another occasion Jesus said, "Do not think that I came to bring peace on the earth; I did not come to bring peace, but a sword" (Matthew 10:34, NASB).

One writer makes the distinction between worldly peace and the peace of Christ this way:

> The kind of peace that the world gives is the peace we experience when for a little time the world happens to be peaceful. It is a peace that lasts for only as long as the peaceful time lasts because as soon as the peaceful time ends, the peace ends with it. The peace that Jesus offers, on the other hand, has nothing to do with the things that are going on at the moment when he offers to give it, which are for the most part tragic and terrible things. It is a profound and inward peace that sees with unflinching clarity the tragic

and terrible things that are happening and yet is not shattered by them . . . because deep beneath all the broken and unholy things that are happening in it even as he speaks, Jesus sees what he calls the Kingdom of God.[2]

So what is this peculiar peace? I believe it is more than we dare hope and pray for, and not as much as we want in this present life. We are restless for our Father's embrace, yet we have a peace now that assures us that someday we will be forever nestled in His lap. Annie Dillard describes restless peace as living in "tranquility and trembling."[3]

Being the selfish, pleasure seekers that we are, too often we embrace the tranquility part without wanting to tremble. We want peace defined on our terms, peace that means lack of conflict and fulfillment of our present desires. While appearing to be more in our control, this is the peace as the world gives and never truly satisfies our souls.

We Hope and Pray

God's peace requires two components, prayer and hope, joined together in love. God's restless peace resonates and grows in us as we live a prayer-centered life. The more we commune with Him, the more we trust His love, the more we act in faith, the more we hope. The apostle Paul captured the interdependence of peace, prayer, and hope in our lives when he addressed the Romans:

> Therefore, since we have been justified through *faith*, we have *peace* with God through our Lord Jesus Christ, through whom we have gained access by faith into this *grace in which we now stand. And we rejoice in the hope of the glory of God. Not only so, but we also rejoice in our sufferings, because we know that suffering produces perseverance; perseverance, character; and character, hope. And hope does not disappoint us, because God has poured out his love into our hearts by the Holy Spirit, whom he has given us.*
> (Romans 5:1-5, emphasis added)

Why does this kind of persevering and hoping and praying sometimes seem so far removed from us? Why is it easier to imagine flying on the space shuttle to the moon than to hope for what He gives so freely? Why does this kind of hoping seem so different from hoping for a winning lottery ticket or a healthy child or enough money to pay the bills?

The difference between the power of hope in God and hope in a lottery ticket depends on its source or power base. I can hope all I want that I can be a world class swimmer who wins Olympic gold, but that kind of hope doesn't have much of a realistic basis, considering my age, lack of training, and body type. Yet hoping in heaven, in the unseen powerful love of my Abba, often feels as remote and removed as winning a gold medal in the breast stroke. What I usually choose to believe in those moments and what we're told consistently by theologians, preachers, and other Christians is that Christ, the manifestation of God's love, is the ultimate reality. I persevere, act in faith, and believe because I hope; I hope because I am loved.

Bottom line we all wrestle with prayer because we all wrestle with hope; it's part of us by virtue of human nature. It's also at the core of our spiritual nature. As Christians we have committed our lives and hearts to live by and for and with hope on a continual, moment-by-moment basis. Many days this hope lurks like a bird escaped from a cage, up near the rafters of our lives. Often Christian hope remains conceptual, theological, rhetorical, and abstract. But the hope of Christianity cannot remain an aloof concept or symbol. The hope which is Christ encompasses and purifies and transcends most of the hope we experience on a daily basis. It is the foundation of the Christian life, the journey of faith with its ups and downs, dry spells, and mountain views. Like the restless peace that comes with it, Christian hope is full of paradox. It is a jewel-like hummingbird weaving in and out of sight in our lives.

Opportunities to hope come daily. I hope to make enough money to pay my bills. I hope to give good gifts to my family. I hope to resist temptations. I hope my wife grows closer to God. I hope my children know the Father's love by the way my wife and I parent them. These daily opportunities to hope become streams of prayer and tributaries of faith. They lead me to a vast sea of hope in Christ. My daily hopes become my prayers, sometimes my disappointments, often my praises.

The eternal hope of Christ compels us to take the risk of faith. In our relationship with Him we risk when we act out of passion and mystery and hope rather than facts and certainties. Ultimately, we hope for the fulfillment of our Father's love in heaven. Otherwise, why should we risk any of our comfort or convenience now?

Paul wrote to the Corinthians: "If only for this life we have hope in Christ, we are to be pitied more than all men" (1 Corinthians 15:19). We must remind ourselves of the source for our hope—Christ. He overcame crucifixion. He is not trapped by death in an eternal cycle of futility. He is not a static, mythic figure. He is the living God in a fleshy body like yours and mine. He sacrificed Himself and restored our ability to relate personally with the Father. Our hope, while defensible, intelligent, even logical, is ultimately not "provable" beyond the experiences of our own hearts. It is there that hope dwells, or not.

While for existentialists there is nobility in the conscious suffering in the face of futility, for followers of Christ there is a consequence in facing the same suffering in what others might perceive as futility. This consequence expresses itself through the prism of faith and becomes the light of God's willful plan shining through life after life after life, down through history.

From the hope and peace we have in Christ, we give ourselves to those around us. We risk without immediately knowing what God is up to. It's enough that He's up to something and that we're privileged to play a small part in it. When we listen to God's Spirit within us, we might send a stranger money to meet an unknown need. We wrangle children on our backs with the unfettered joy of a bronco. Instead of channel surfing through another sit-com or ball game, we close our doors and shut our blinds and get down on our hands and knees and bow to the living God. We let down our defenses and speak our deepest heart fears to another and allow him or her to speak to us and hold us. We risk. We hope. We pray. We experience His peace, and this pattern of growth continues.

Enduring the Present

When we commit ourselves to Jesus, we kindle a hope in something so much greater than ourselves and the often feeble hopes we become accustomed to. We are awakened by the Spirit dwelling in us. Yet hope in God means that we won't always get our way, be comfortable, or understand what our Father is doing. We will endure the middle ground of being in the process of sanctification—Christ has already died for us and our relationship with our Abba Father is restored. However, when we accept this gift of Christ, we enter into an ongoing process. We move toward Christ, toward God, without reaching the fulfillment of such sanctification in this lifetime. We will not arrive at heaven on earth—we will only have glimpses, C. S. Lewis's "shadowlands," that stir up in us what we are destined to become and enjoy—Christ's likeness. We will be like Him.

When we buy into the fallacy that the Christian life serves as blissful anesthetic to the pain of a fallen, selfish world of people like ourselves, we set ourselves up. We either pretend life is easier and better than it is, at the expense of our integrity, honesty, and internal emotional landscape, or we become cynical, disillusioned, disenfranchised people who are continually on the cusp of chucking our faith altogether. While these are extreme generalities, and we float and bounce somewhere between them, they honestly reflect the main channels most of us experience. Living out of hope has as much to do with our struggles and failures as it does our blessings and triumphs.

As I've tried to illustrate throughout this book, I cannot write about prayer and hope without connecting it to my life, without showing you scenes from my story. Let me tell you about the prayer that has made the most difference in my life and the restless peace that accompanied it and continues to grow. Let me tell you why I hope.

Because of my parents' loving foresight, I attended the only private school in our small, rural Tennessee community. It happened to be a parochial school run by the surprisingly large community of Roman Catholics in our county. As one of only two non-Catholics in my class, I received a glorious, additional education during the daily mass we attended and the weekly catechism class. However, on Sundays I attended the First Baptist Church of my small town, where the Bible was preached diligently, if not passionately, by a large man with crooked glasses and the same navy suit week after week. The two faith systems seemed to have little in common, and perhaps this was reinforced by my dear grandmother's concerns that I would pray to "Mother Mary" during the school week.

Mail-Order Bride of Christ

I continued to walk the tightrope between these two divergent views of Christian faith. By age twelve, I went through the prescribed steps of becoming a Christian in my Protestant church, and while my mind understood most of the basics, I grasped none of it in my bones. My life did not change. My heart was as sealed to hope as Lazarus' tomb before Jesus showed up. Over the next years I survived the terrible teens and finally made my great escape to the state university. By the time I was a junior, I had made about as big a mess of my life as any of us can.

I had just broken up from a smothering two-year relationship with a hometown girl. I didn't know what to do with my life vocationally. I was disillusioned with the fraternity I had joined where the depth of brotherhood never transcended locker-room banter. I was drinking regularly (like when the sun went down). Finally, on a cold, starry night in January I drank myself into oblivion and considered taking my body there, too, by locking myself in a bathroom with a razor blade.

After I realized that I didn't want to die, I began seeking. This led me to the small Catholic student center on campus where I soon found myself every afternoon. In the cool dark of its tiny stained-glass chapel, I would sit alone and sort through my pain. The candle of the sacrament would flicker beneath the outstretched, crucified man above me. It didn't feel like prayer as I was accustomed to it, but looking back, it was the most holy, sincere communication I may have ever had with God. The dam of my emotions finally burst one day and I wept the way only desperate people in silent abandonment before God can weep. I felt very small, a compact shell of soul barnacled to this life that I was intent on destroying up till then. I whispered, "Please, do something. Please be real and please take this tangled mess of my life and save me from myself." I asked for much more than that. I asked for the revelation of His presence, for guidance, for a sign even. I asked for it all.

It was quiet and cool and I felt relieved, still uncertain about what I had asked for. There was no rainbow outside as I left the chapel and proceeded to go to class and then to a late lunch. In the cafeteria two young men asked to share my table, even though the place was no longer crowded. They sipped Cokes nervously and tried to make small talk about sports. Finally, they ventured, "Do you happen to go to church?"

"Yeah," I said, "I go to John XXXIII here on campus." *Oh no, Jesus freaks*, I thought to myself. That explained their fidgety attempt to make my acquaintance. I had already rebuffed countless churches, parachurch groups, and attractive cults who seemed to target me relentlessly.

"So, uh, you're Catholic?" the tall, lanky one asked.

"No, it's just where I go." I crumpled my napkin over the remains of my sandwich and began to stand up.

"So would you consider yourself a Christian?" the older one asked. He wore tortoiseshell glasses and a buttoned-down oxford, obviously the leader, the staff guy.

"Sure, I guess so. Listen, I gotta get going." I rose from the table.

"Would you be willing to talk for just a couple of minutes? We just want to talk about your beliefs, you know. What it's like to know Christ personally."

I hated to hurt them. I couldn't say no; I would just remain polite and cool and claim I had to be somewhere soon. And then it clicked, almost audibly, one of those rare moments when the clock stops and the hairs on your neck shoot up, and you simply know something extraordinary is happening, is wooing you. *What if this were my sign? What if God was using these two guys to present Himself to me?* I thought to myself. *Could it be?* I had to at least give Him the benefit of the doubt and listen to what they had to say.

They introduced themselves as Kevin and Tad and dived right into asking me questions that led quite predictably into a little booklet they happened to have handy. I listened, though. I had ears to hear that day, eyes to see. I took in what they said and looked behind their eyes for some flicker of passion to go with what they were saying. They convinced me only because He loved me right then in the silly, earnestness of my request. I agreed to meet with them the following day. Until then I promised to read the first three chapters of John's gospel and to think about what I desired more than anything.

I ended up that night back in the quiet little chapel, consummating the relationship I had dared ask for only hours earlier. I knelt and embraced and entrusted myself to a God whom I supposedly knew quite a lot about in theory, yet barely knew at all personally. The commitment encompassed all the exhilaration and fear of marrying someone I had read about in the personals but had not yet met face-to-face. A kind of mail-order bride of Christ, I suppose.

Lifetime Conversation

To say that experience has changed my life underrates both the event and its consequent impact, rippling through the brook of time, seen and unseen, affecting who I am and how I live. Certainly I don't have the Christian life and prayer all figured out. Most days, I don't always know why I hope, but along the way I've quit asking as frequently as I once did. I keep praying because He loves me. I keep praying because I love Him. I can hope nothing higher than that you pray for the same reasons and that you pray as only you can.

What is prayer? Prayer is the egg white of the gold yolk of our lives, dribbling out, nourishing, protecting, guarding, connecting. Prayer is the white water of grace and joy and love breaking out of the shells of our selfish hearts. What is restless peace? It's a collection of moments, many of which will be repetitious — waking, eating, walking, working, driving, sleeping. It is our conversation with God in these moments, the times of loving, of sitting very still, our eyes lighting on a purple bloom of wild oleander outside our window, of pulling someone close and loving them and smelling the sweet human smell of their hair, of talking out loud to an unseen God who shows Himself because He cannot hide His love.

Prayer is welcoming our Father's presence into a lifetime conversation with our hearts. Calling Him up throughout the hour, day, week, month, year of our lives like calling up your best friend, or your father or mother, or the person you love most in the world. Finally, prayer is our ultimate conversation of knowing and being known, of loving and being loved. This communion with our Father sustains us for this lifetime and whets our appetites for the next. We talk long-distance now until that day, that brightest moment of our existence, when we hear

Him speak inches away from us, when we see the glory of His face. That day our prayers finally find the truest expression of our heart's longing: a new language of love, an eternal psalm of praise to our dearest One.

Questions for Prayer and Reflection

1. How have you experienced God's "restless peace" in the past? How does praying increase this kind of peace while also increasing your desire for the One who gives it?

2. Think back to the time when you first began your relationship with Christ. How does your present prayer life differ from the way you prayed then? What have you learned since then about communicating with God?

3. How would you describe the kind of peace that Jesus, through the Holy Spirit, brings into our lives versus the peace of the world? Recall times when you've experienced each of these and compare them.

4. How has your view of prayer changed since beginning this book? Why?

5. What continues to bother you about prayer? Consider asking your Abba Father to reveal Himself to you, despite areas of concern that remain.

Father, my heart is full of so many things, so many desires and longings, fears and anxieties. Please burn through to my heart with your love in ways I can't imagine. Kindle in me a holy fire, a passion unlike the mediocrity I accept so easily in my faith. Continue to speak to me and to show me how to speak to you. Reveal yourself in all that I do and in all those I love. Father, teach me to pray, through our Lord Jesus. Amen.

NOTES

Introduction: Starting from Zero

1. Richard J. Foster, *Prayer: Finding the Heart's True Home* (San Francisco: Harper, 1992), p. 9.
2. C. S. Lewis, *Letters to Malcolm: Chiefly on Prayer* (New York: Harcourt Brace, 1964), p. 22.

Chapter One: Beyond Busyness

1. George Dawson, *Communion of Saints: Prayers of the Famous*, ed. Horton Davies (Grand Rapids: Eerdmans, 1990), p. 91.

Chapter Two: Praying in the Dark

1. Philip Yancey, "Why Not Now?" *Christianity Today*, February 1996, America Online: ctfeb96mrj6T21126125.
2. Dan Allender and Tremper Longman, III, *Cry of the Soul* (Colorado Springs: NavPress, 1994), p. 142.
3. Philip Yancey, *Disappointment With God* (Grand Rapids: Zondervan, 1988), p. 165.
4. Yancey, p. 173.
5. Henri Nouwen, in *HarperCollins Book of Prayer*, ed. Robert Van de Weyer (San Francisco: Harper, 1993), p. 274.

Chapter Three: Afraid to Hope

1. Langston Hughes, "Harlem." From *Collected Poems* by Langston Hughes. Copyright © 1994 by the Estate of Langston Hughes. Reprinted by permission of Alfred A. Knopf, Inc.
2. Perry D. LeFevre, *The Prayers of Kierkegaard* (Chicago: Phoenix/University of Chicago Press, 1963), p. 40.

Chapter Four: Finding Our Voice

1. Sören Kierkegaard, {The Prayers of Soren Kierkegaard}, ed. Perry D. LeFevre (Chicago: Phoenix/University of Chicag Press, 1963), p. 342..
2. Frederick Buechner, *Wishful Thinking: A Theological ABC* (New York: Harper & Row, 1973), p. 70.
3. Henri Nouwen, *With Open Hands* (Notre Dame, Ind.: Ave Maria Press, 1995), pp. 12-13.
4. Brother Lawrence, *The Practice of the Presence of God* (Springdale, Penn.: Whitaker, 1982), p. 26.
5. Brother Lawrence, "An Habitual Sense of God's Presence," in *Devotional Classics*, ed.

Richard J. Foster and James Bryan Smith (San Francisco: Harper, 1993), p. 83.

6. My brief mention in this chapter cannot do justice to Brother Lawrence's experience and writings. So, if you haven't discovered *The Practice of the Presence of God*, I urge you to read it. If you have read it, perhaps now is the time to read it again, to experience the timelessness of its message once again. Either way, consider what it would look like for you to choose to remember God in the midst of washing dishes, filing reports, bidding contracts, changing diapers, taking exams, parking cars, preparing sermons, bussing tables.

7. Alice Walker, "Everyday Use," *In Love & Trouble* (New York: Harvest/Harcourt Brace Jovanovich, 1973), pp. 57-58.

8 For a more lengthy treatment of these temptations and their significance, see Chapter Two in my book *A Repentant Heart* (Colorado Springs: NavPress, 1995).

9. Annie Dillard, *Teaching a Stone to Talk* (New York: Harper Perennial, 1983), p. 25.

10. Madeleine L'Engle, *The Weather of the Heart* (Wheaton, Ill.: Shaw, 1978), p. 60. "Word," Luci Shaw, copyright 1978. Used by permission of Harold Shaw Publishers, Wheaton, IL 60189.

11.Thomas à Kempis, "Solitude," in *Disciplines for the Inner Life*, ed. Bob Benson and Michael W. Benson (Nashville: Generoux/Nelson, 1989), p. 59.

Chapter Five: Operating Instructions

1. James Joyce (1882–1941) was an Irish writer best known for works such as *Portrait of the Artist as a Young Man* and *Ulysses*. His novels are characterized by stream-of-consciousness and often contain mythological and religious allusions.

2. *Bartlett's Familiar Quotations*, sixteenth edition, ed. John Bartlett and Justin Kaplan (Boston: Little, Brown, & Co., 1992), p. 127.

3. Richard Foster, *Prayer: Finding the Heart's True Home* (San Francisco: Harper, 1992), p. 185.

4. Paul Duke, "Praying With a Sideward Glance," *Christian Century*, 11 October 1995, p. 923.

5. Ray Stedman in *Disciplines for the Inner Life*, ed. Bob Benson and Michael W. Benson (Nashville: Generoux/Nashville, 1989), p. 240.

Chapter Six: Other Spokes on the Wheel

1. Richard Foster, *Prayer: Finding the Heart's True Home* (San Francisco: Harper, 1992), p. 199.

2. Henri Nouwen, *With Open Hands* (Notre Dame, Ind.: Ave Maria Press, 1995), pp. 86-87.

3. Michael A. Fletcher, "Christian Coalition Pledges Aid," The *Denver Post*, 19 June 1996, p. 2A.

4. *The New Book of Christian Prayers*, ed. Tony Castle (New York: Crossroad, 1987), p. 221.

Chapter Seven: True Confessions

1. Taken from *Writing the River* copyright 1994 by Luci Shaw. Used by permission of Pinon Press. For copies call 1-800-366-7788.

2. Frederick Buechner, *Wishful Thinking: A Theological ABC* (New York: Harper & Row, 1973), p. 15.

3. Ron Hansen, *Atticus* (New York: HarperCollins, 1996), p. 8.
4. Annie Dillard, *Pilgrim at Tinker Creek* (New York: Harper & Row, 1974), p. 268.
5. Madeleine L'Engle, *Walking on Water: Reflections on Faith & Art* (Wheaton, Ill.: Shaw, 1978), p. 180.
6. *The Book of Common Prayer* (New York: Seabury Press, 1979), p. 352.

Chapter Eight: Praying for Rain
1. Mark Twain, *The Adventures of Huckleberry Finn* (New York: Modern Library, 1985), p. 29.
2. C. S. Lewis, *Letters to Malcolm: Chiefly on Prayer* (New York: Harcourt Brace, 1964), p. 58.
3. Ole Hallesby, *Prayer* (Minneapolis: Augsburg, 1994), p. 121.
4. Frederick Buechner, *Wishful Thinking: A Theological ABC* (New York: Harper & Row, 1973), p. 71.
5. Annie Dillard, *Pilgrim at Tinker Creek* (New York: Harper & Row, 1974), p. 269.
6. Sören Kierkegaard, *The Prayers of Sören Kierkegaard*, ed. Perry D. LeFevre (Chicago: Phoenix/University of Chicago Press, 1963), p. 342.
7. Dillard, *Holy the Firm*, pp. 57-58.
8. In *Communion of Saints: Prayers of the Famous*, ed. Davies Horton (Grand Rapids: Eerdmans, 1990), p. 32.
9. Thomas à Kempis, *The Imitation of Christ* (Grand Rapids: Clarion/Zondervan, 1983), p. 94.

Chapter Nine: Pied Beauty
1. In *Prayers*, ed. Peter Washington (New York: Knopf, 1995), p. 100.
2. In *New Book of Christian Prayers*, ed. Tony Castle (New York: Crossroad, 1983), p. 62.
3. Richard J. Foster, *Prayer: Finding the Heart's True Home* (San Francisco: Harper, 1992), p. 83.
4. Teresa of Avila in *New Book of Christian Prayers* ed. Tony Castle (New York: Crossroad, 1983), p. 85.
5. Brevard Childs, *Introduction to Old Testament as Scripture* (Philadelphia: Fortress Press, 1979), p. 518.
6. Eugene Peterson, *Answering God: The Psalms as Tools for Prayer* (San Francisco: Harper, 1989), pp. 121-122.
7. Robert Robinson, *The Hymnal for Worship & Celebration*, (Waco: Word Music, 1986) p. 2.
8. In *Amazing Grace: 366 Inspiring Hymn Stories for Daily Devotions*, ed. Kenneth W. Osbeck (Grand Rapids: Kregel, 1990), p. 343
9. Dillard, *Pilgrim at Tinker Creek*, p. 270.
10. Dillard, p. 271.
11. In *Prayers*, ed.Peter Washington (New York: Knopf, 1995), p. 100.

Chapter Ten: Living Our Prayers
1. Nouwen, *Creative Ministry* (New York: Bantam/Doubleday, 1991).
2. Brennan Manning, *Abba's Child* (Colorado Springs: NavPress, 1994), p. 61.
3. C. S. Lewis, *Letters to Malcolm: Chiefly on Prayer* (New York: Harcourt Brace, 1964), p. 43.

4. Paraphrased responses from *The Message* by Eugene Peterson, Matthew 4:1-11.
5. Frederick Buechner, *The Longing for Home: Recollections and Reflections* (San Francisco: Harper, 1996), p. 127.
6. Hannah Whitall Smith, *The Christian's Secret of a Happy Life* (Old Tappan, N.J.: Revell, 1952), p. 185.
7. Eugene Peterson, *A Long Obedience in the Same Direction* (Downers Grove, Ill.: InterVarsity, 1980), p. 61.
8. In *Devotional Classics*, ed. Richard Foster and James Bryan Smith (San Francisco: Harper, 1993), pp. 27-29.
9. Manning, *Abba's Child*, p. 50.
10. In *Communion of Saints: Prayers of the Famous*, ed. Davies Horton (Grand Rapids: Eerdmans, 1990), p. 70.

Chapter Eleven: Hearing God's Voice
1. Dallas Willard, *In Search of Guidance* (New York: Zondervan/HarperCollins, 1993), p. 97.
2. F. B. Meyer, *The Secret of Guidance*, pp. 14-15, quoted in Willard, p. 182.
3. Frederick Buechner, *The Alphabet of Grace* (San Francisco: Harper & Row, 1970), p. 3.
4. Buechner, *The Alphabet of Grace*, p. 12.
5. Buechner, *The Final Beast* (San Francisco: Harper & Row, 1965), pp. 176-178.
6. Willard, *In Search of Guidance*, p. 186.
7. Brennan Manning, *Abba's Child* (Colorado Springs: NavPress, 1994), p. 64.
8. Christina Rosetti, "Behold a Shaking" in *Women in Praise of the Sacred*, ed. Jane Hirschfield (New York: HarperCollins, 1994), p. 190.
9. Charles Wesley, "With Thee Conversing," in *HarperCollins Book of Prayers*, ed. Robert Van de Weyer (San Francisco: Harper, 1993).

Chapter Twelve: Restless Peace
1. Anne Lamott, *Operating Instructions: A Journal of My Son's First Year* (New York: Fawcett Columbine, 1993), pp. 220-221.
2. Frederick Buechner, *The Longing for Home: Recollections and Reflections* (San Francisco: Harper, 1996), pp. 74-75.
3. Annie Dillard, *Pilgrim at Tinker Creek*, p. 269.

AUTHOR

DUDLEY J. DELFFS is a writer and English instructor at Colorado Christian University. He also serves as fiction editor of the literary journal *Mars Hill Review*. He earned B.A. and M.A. degrees in English from the University of Tennessee and an M.A. in counseling from Colorado Christian University. He has published poetry and short fiction in various journals and is the author of *Forgiving August*, a novel (Piñon Press, 1993); and *A Repentant Heart*, a non-fictional book on spiritual transformation (NavPress, 1995). He lives in Littleton, Colorado, with his wife, Dotti, and daughters, Mary Elise and Annie.